# ASSET VALUATION

## AND

# INCOME DETERMINATION

A Consideration of the Alternatives

# ACCOUNTING PUBLICATIONS OF SCHOLARS BOOK CO.

## ROBERT R. STERLING, EDITOR

Sidney S. Alexander, et al., *Five Monographs on Business Income*

Frank Sewall Bray, *The Accounting Mission*

Raymond J. Chambers, *Accounting, Evaluation and Economic Behavior*

Arthur Lowes Dickinson, *Accounting Practice and Procedure*

John B. Geijsbeek, *Ancient Double-Entry Bookkeeping*

Henry Rand Hatfield, *Accounting: Its Principles and Problems*

Bishop Carlton Hunt (Editor), *George Oliver May: Twenty-Five Years of Accounting Responsibility*

Kenneth MacNeal, *Truth in Accounting*

George O. May, *Financial Accounting: A Distillation of Experience*

Paul D. Montagna, *Certified Public Accounting: A Sociological View of a Profession in Change*

William A. Paton, *Accounting Theory*

W. Z. Ripley, *Main Street and Wall Street*

DR Scott, *The Cultural Significance of Accounts*

Charles E. Sprague, *The Philosophy of Accounts*

George Staubus, *A Theory of Accounting to Investors*

Robert R. Sterling (Editor), *Asset Valuation and Income Determination: A Consideration of the Alternatives*

Robert R. Sterling (Editor), *Institutional Issues in Public Accounting*

Robert R. Sterling (Editor), *Research Methodology in Accounting*

Study Group on Business Income, *Changing Concepts of Business Income*

# ASSET VALUATION

## AND

# INCOME DETERMINATION

## A Consideration of the Alternatives

Papers Given at a Symposium
Held at the
School of Business
University of Kansas
May 1970

*Edited by Robert R. Sterling*

SCHOLARS BOOK CO.
4431 Mt. Vernon
Houston, Texas 77006 USA

STANDARD BOOK NUMBER: 0-914348-11-6
LIBRARY OF CONGRESS CATALOG NUMBER: 73-160580
MANUFACTURED IN THE UNITED STATES OF AMERICA

# PREFACE

The debate over the proper method of valuing assets and measuring income is not new to the accounting literature, but it has become increasingly intense in recent years. The major schools of thought that have emerged are: (1) historical cost and realized income; (2) replacement costs and business income; (3) current cash equivalents and realizable income; and (4) discounted cash flows and economic income. As is made clear by the papers, these schools are not mutually exclusive in that each school borrows from the others at certain points. In addition, the list is not exhaustive. However, these seem to be the main contenders at the present time.

The idea of the Symposium was to bring together representatives from each of the schools so that they could present and defend their positions and then, in turn, join in the discussion of the other positions. It was hoped that this would result in the resolution of some of the differences between the schools and highlight the reasons for the differences that were not resolved. Of equal importance was the idea of involving practitioners in the debate. It was hoped that the comments of the practitioners would be beneficial to the development of theory and that the comments of the professors would be beneficial to the development of practice.

Instead of trying to summarize the papers, and perhaps thereby display my own views and biases, I will let the authors speak for themselves. The organization of the papers in this volume follows generally the way in which they were presented at the Symposium. The first four papers are presentations of the positions of the four schools of thought, followed by a separate response to each paper. The next three papers are critical assessments of the four schools. Both days of the Symposium were concluded by a dinner speech, which are the final two papers in this volume.

The Symposium and publication of this book were made possible by a grant from the Touche Ross Foundation. I appreciate not only the grant but also the spirit with which it was given. I am especially indebted to Donald J. Bevis for his wise counsel and many courtesies.

Robert R. Sterling

October 1970
University of Kansas
Lawrence, Kansas

# CONTENTS

# 1

# A Defense for Historical Cost Accounting

*by* Yuji Ijiri

CARNEGIE-MELLON UNIVERSITY

## I. Introduction

IT IS truly remarkable that historical cost accounting has been the principal methodology of accounting over several centuries. Unfortunately, however, familiarity often breeds contempt, and attacks on historical cost accounting have been launched from various corners of business and accounting, especially since the beginning of the second half of this century.

The argument that I am going to present in this paper in defense of historical cost accounting is addressed not only to those who attempt to eliminate it completely from the field of accounting but also to those who recognize the significance of historical cost accounting only to a very limited extent. However, it is not addressed to those who evaluate highly the contribution by historical cost accounting but nonetheless advocate the need for improving it and supplementing it by other procedures. I, myself, do not consider historical cost accounting to have all the answers for the whole field of accounting. Nevertheless, I do believe that the contribution made by historical cost accounting is really significant and that it will continue to make significant contributions to business in the future as well.

It is difficult to recognize the value of something to which we are very much accustomed. However, if the best way to recognize the value of the air is to try to stop breathing or to move into a highly polluted area, perhaps we can apply the same principle and imagine

1

what the business world might look like without historical cost accounting.

In the next section, I shall present the accounting practices of five hypothetical countries, A through E. The role of historical cost accounting will be increased gradually as we move from Country A through Country E. Then in Section III, I shall summarize my argument for historical cost accounting imbedded in the accounting practices in these countries.

## II. A Defense for Historical Cost

In order to obtain some insights into the significant role that has been played by historical cost accounting, let us consider what might happen if we substituted current cost accounting for historical cost accounting. I use current cost accounting because it is the alternative to historical cost accounting which has been most strongly advocated. However, a similar type of argument as the one presented in this section is also applicable to other kinds of proposed alternatives to historical cost accounting.

The firms in Country A do not keep any records on the historical flows of resources. Instead, the accounting practices of this country require that a firm take a physical inventory of all assets and liabilities at the end of each year and evaluate them at the current costs. Income for the year is then calculated as the difference in the net worth at the end of the year and the net worth at the beginning of the year, after adjusting for capital transactions (new stock issues, dividends, etc.). The historical records of the resource flows are not required since the history of how resources came under a firm's control (e.g., how much was paid for the resources) is totally irrelevant in the current cost valuation.

The investors in this country are completely at the mercy of the management, because they are only told the results of the operations of the firm with no recourse to check how the results have been produced. The management can spend the firm's resources in any way they want without leaving any trace of where the resources came from and where they went, since in this country, past records are considered to be of no interest. Instead, a considerable effort is made in each firm at the year-end to list every asset and liability of the firm and evaluate them at their year-end prices. A balance sheet is then prepared at current cost and the income for the year is calculated as stated above.

Undoubtedly, this is the most primitive way of recording and reporting in current cost accounting. However, even in this balance sheet method of calculating income, if the valuation method is based on historical cost, the investors can implicitly impose the condition on the firm that historical records of transactions be kept, since without records of historical resource flows it is not possible to evaluate resources in historical costs. This automatic control feature of historical cost accounting is completely lacking in Country A.

While current cost accounting does not have the resource control feature imbedded in its valuation method, the resource control system can be initiated in addition to the year-end valuation. Let us introduce such a control system in Country B while retaining the current cost valuation method.

The accounting practice in Country B is slightly more civilized. The valuation method used in this country is also the current cost basis as in Country A, but in Country B, it is required to keep records in physical units on the increase and the decrease in every type of resource. The firm takes a physical inventory of all assets and liabilities at the end of each year, but unlike Country A, the physical inventory is only a means of verifying the accuracy of the records rather than the sole basis for preparing the financial statements.

The reason that the records are kept in physical units is that current costs change over time and the year-end prices cannot be anticipated during the year. Historical costs are considered to be of no value, hence, they are completely eliminated from the records.

Although in this country it is required to keep records for changes in each type of resource in physical units, it is not required to keep records on how much of the resources (inputs) were spent to obtain how much of the other resources (outputs). For example, it is required to keep a stock ledger indicating in the respective physical units the balance and changes in each item in the inventories, and to keep a cash ledger for every cash receipt and disbursement. It is not required to keep a record on how much was paid for materials, since it is irrelevant for the current cost valuation. In other words, records on the balance and changes in each resource type are kept independently from those in other resource types in a single-entry fashion, instead of relating inputs and outputs as observed in the double-entry book-keeping system. In this sense, firms in this country do not have records of "transactions," as currently exist in the United States and else-where, although records of every change in every type of asset and liability are properly kept.

This lack of transaction records in Country B presents a serious weakness in resource management and control not only in purchases, but also in production, in sales and in all other activities of a firm. Note that such a situation cannot occur if historical cost accounting is used. When a firm receives 100 units of materials, it must determine how much money has been or is going to be paid for those materials, since otherwise their historical cost cannot be determined. Similarly, when 50 units of finished goods are produced, a firm must determine how much material was used for the finished goods in order to de-termine their historical cost. Thus, every increase and decrease in resources is "chained" by means of the input-output relationship in historical cost accounting. The double-entry bookkeeping system offers an effective means of recording this relationship.[1]

Of course, it is possible to chain the changes in resources in physical units, and there is no reason why the double-entry bookkeeping sys-tem cannot be utilized to accommodate such a transaction as

Dr. Materials                                      100 units
   Cr. Cash                                          $4,000

although the equality of the debit entry and the credit entry is no longer maintained.[2] Similarly, there is no reason why some sort of estimate of the year-end current costs cannot be used as a basis of recording as in standard cost accounting, although it would become necessary to set up such estimates or standards for all kinds of assets, including fixed assets. But, the fundamental difference between his-torical cost accounting and current cost accounting is that in the former, the chaining of inputs and outputs is the basis for the valua-tion, while in the latter, such an automatic control feature is missing.

At the very minimum, the significance of the custodianship func-tion of historical cost accounting seems unquestionable. Actually, the

---

[1] See Yuji Ijiri, *The Foundations of Accounting Measurement* (New York: Prentice-Hall, 1967), Chapter 5 on the inseparable relationship between the double-entry bookkeeping system and historical cost valuation.

[2] *Ibid.*

function of accounting in controlling the resources of a firm is the most fundamental one with which accounting began several centuries ago. Since then, the role of accounting has been expanded considerably. But, the important question now is whether the custodianship function has become insignificant. Knowing that millions of investors are relying upon the custodianship function of accounting when they invest in a firm, how can one discuss accounting without considering this important function?

However, the significance of historical cost accounting is far from being limited to the custodianship function, as we shall see in the next example.

Let us now observe the accounting practices in Country C. Here, the importance of historical cost accounting in resource control is fully recognized, and it is required to keep records on the resource flows, based on the historical costs. However, for the purpose of income distribution in the form of dividends, bonuses to officers and employers, income taxes, refunds to customers of a firm in a regulated industry, etc., it is required to base the determination of income on the current cost method of valuation.

Here, the income figure is used not just as information but as a means of solving conflicts of interest in income distribution. Therefore, the process of income determination must be carried out in the least disputable manner. Otherwise, tremendous pressures will be put on accountants, and the process of income determination will become a process of political negotiations rather than a process of systematic calculations. A flood of law suits will arise out of disputes over income figures, and the social cost of accounting will become phenomenal.

It is extremely important that the basis of income determination be least disputable if the income figure is to be used as a basis of income distribution. Unfortunately, however, accountants in Country C will find current cost income (income determined under the current cost valuation) far more disputable and therefore less suitable as a basis for income distribution than historical cost income.

Current cost accounting is based on contemplated transactions. In order to determine current cost income, it is first necessary to set up a method of determining uniquely which contemplated transaction should be used as a basis of valuation. This is because there are numerous transactions that may be contemplated with respect to the replacement or the disposal of a given resource. Various outside offers may be received, market prices at various domestic and foreign markets may be quoted. Which alternative should be used as a basis? The highest, or the lowest, or an average? How should the search area, to get offers or find prices, be determined? Notice that it is not enough to determine whether a contemplated transaction is reasonable, since in many cases there is more than one contemplated transaction that is considered to be reasonable. In order to avoid disputes over the income figure, there must be a means of determining a unique transaction among all transactions that may be contemplated with respect to a given resource.

Historical cost accounting avoids this problem, since it is based on the actual transaction that was chosen by the firm. Of course, both in historical cost accounting and in current cost accounting, there is room for disputes over the interpretation of the financial effects of the transaction. But, at least the former is less disputable than the latter by not having the problem of selecting one out of numerous transactions that can be contemplated.

The second factor which makes current cost income more disputable than historical cost income is the non-additivity of current costs. The historical cost of Resource A and Resource B is *by definition* the sum of the historical cost of Resource A and Resource B. If A is purchased at $10 and B at $15, the historical cost of A and B is defined to be $25.

This additivity does not exist in current cost valuation, insofar as the price of a resource is not necessarily equal to the sum of the prices of its components. If the current cost of Resource A is $20 and Resource B is $30 but that of A and B together is $60, should we use $50 or $60 as the current cost of Resource A and Resource B? Similarly, in evaluating a large quantity of merchandise, the price for the entire lot can be quite different from the sum of the prices for the sublots, even if the lot consists of only one homogeneous product due to quantity discounts, ease or difficulty in purchasing or selling a large lot, etc. Also, the component-by-component valuation of a plant can be quite different from the valuation of the plant as a whole. What is more serious is the problem that the component-by-component evaluation of the assets of a firm or its subsidiary can be considerably different from the valuation of the firm or its subsidiary as an organism. This problem of determining the level of aggregation at which resources in the firm (or the firm itself) should be evaluated is a serious one that must be resolved in order to avoid disputes over current cost income.

However, there is a diametrically opposite problem in historical cost accounting. Instead of the above aggregation problem in historical cost accounting, the problem is one of disaggregation, or allocation. Suppose that Resources A and B are purchased together for $20, but at the end of the year the firm had only Resource A. How much of the $20 should be assigned to Resource A? Depreciation is a typical problem of this kind. However, accountants have devised many methods, however arbitrary they may be, by which such allocations are carried out objectively. Furthermore, it must be noted that disaggregation problems occur only when resources purchased originally as a group are split among periods, departments, or products, whereas the aggregration problem in current cost accounting discussed above always occurs. It even occurs when only one kind of resource is at issue, as in the homogeneous product case mentioned above.

Therefore, to those who think that current cost accounting eliminates the messy problem of depreciation and other joint cost allocations, it must be pointed out that in current cost accounting there is the much messier problem of aggregation and that any rules derived to specify the aggregation level (e.g., a plant should be evaluated as a whole, but a subsidiary should be evaluated as the sum of the values of its assets) are just as arbitrary as the depreciation methods.

The third problem which makes current cost income less suitable for use in income distribution than historical cost income is the difficulty in specifying and verifying the level of likelihood that a contemplated transaction may actually take place. Nobody has proposed to evaluate assets of a U.S. firm based on the market prices in China when everybody knows that such a deal can never take place. How likely should a contemplated transaction be and how should the likelihood be verified? It would be easy for firms to exchange phony offers in order to help each other get a favorable income figure, unless there were a safeguard against such chicanery. But how could one verify whether an offer made by Firm B to purchase or rebuild a plant of Firm A at $1 million was bona fide or phony unless the deal had actually been consummated? If current cost income is used as a basis for income distribution, endless disputes would arise over the seriousness of such offers.

Attempts to remedy these three problems in current cost accounting may perhaps be worthwhile if it can be shown that current cost income leads to more "equitable" distribution of income than historical cost income. This is extremely difficult to show. On the contrary, historical cost accounting, which refuses to recognize holding gains and losses, seems to be more in line with the fundamental spirit of the law aimed at solving conflicts of interest, namely, the maintenance of the status quo until changes (in income) are proven necessary beyond any reasonable doubt. Contemplation alone is not subject to reward or punishment by law regardless of its content, because it is too weak a foundation for a legal relationship among interested parties. To stand the heat and pressure of legal disputes over income distribution, the realizable income concept is far too weak compared with the realized income concept.

From the examples of accounting practices in Countries A, B and C, it is obvious that historical cost accounting has been and will be the most effective method of accounting in the area of resource control and distribution. Accounting has two fundamentally different functions to perform; one function is to protect the equity of interested parties of a firm and the other is to provide relevant data to decision makers (inside and outside the firm) to help them make decisions on resource allocation. Accounting oriented toward the former function is called *equity accounting*, and accounting oriented toward the latter function is called *operational accounting*.[3]

Obviously, more rigorous rules are required in equity accounting than in operational accounting. The rules of the latter emphasize the relevance and timing of data in relation to the decision at the expense of verification and objectivity. In fact, it is of secondary importance whether financial data produced in equity accounting are properly supplied to interested parties, insofar as the parties can trust accountants that their system has been operating properly. In equity accounting, the primary importance is the system itself and not the financial data per se.

The significance of equity accounting should not be undercut by the recent shift of emphasis toward decision making and operational

---

[3] *Ibid.*

accounting. For the proper functioning of our economy, it is essential to have a system which assures the investors not only that the total resources invested in the firm are properly controlled (the custodianship function) but also that each investor's share is properly protected from other investors and other interested parties of the firm. Equity accounting is aimed at exactly this objective. This is the area in which accounting has traditionally developed. Although operational accounting is playing a more and more important role in business, the significance of equity accounting and the central role of historical cost accounting in equity accounting should be fully recognized.

In the above argument, the area in which I believe historical cost accounting has played and will play an indispensable role was expanded from custodianship accounting to equity accounting. I would now like to expand it further to include at least a part of operational accounting, since I do believe that information provided by historical cost accounting is useful for management and investment decisions, although I fully realize the need for additional types of information. In order to highlight the contribution of historical cost accounting in operational accounting, let us imagine Country D in which historical cost data are completely barred for use by management and investors.

In Country D, equity accounting is based on historical cost accounting, but accountants in this country believe that historical cost data are useful only in equity accounting and are of no use for decision making purposes. They even consider such data to be misleading if provided to the management and the public. As a result, the records prepared in equity accounting are shielded from everybody except a special audit agency of the government which thoroughly audits the records of each firm and issues a report. Financial statements prepared under historical cost accounting are made available only to the audit agency. The management and the public are given only the audit report, which includes the income figure and an opinion by the audit agency that proper records were maintained and the income figure was derived properly. This income figure is then used for all purposes of income distribution.

Although the management and the public do not receive any historial cost data other than the income figure verified by the audit agency, they are well provided with current cost data. Financial statements prepared on the current cost basis are published regularly and made available to the public to help them make investment and other decisions. The management is also provided with a set of current cost data whenever necessary, although historical cost data are barred entirely in operational accounting, since they are considered to be misleading or at least of no use.

What would happen in a country like this? I can offer only my conjecture of what would happen if historical cost data were eliminated entirely from the business world.

Vicious complaints would arise, first from the management and then from the public. The management would argue strongly against the accountants who hold that historical cost data are useless. They would argue that management is a dynamic process which requires a careful study of the past in order to predict the future. To substitute current cost data for historical cost data is like wiping out their past experiences. They would want to know the price of the material at the last purchase so that they can compare it with the price they have to pay presently. Historical cost data provide useful information, they would say, not only when they are compared with current cost data, but also when they are compared with other historical cost data, as in the analysis of trends, seasonal cycles, comparisons with other departments or firms, etc. Of course, they would not deny the usefulness of current cost data, but they would be opposed to the idea that historical cost data are useless.

Complaints from the public on the financial statements under the current cost basis would be raised for a different reason. As in the case of Country C, current cost data offer much more room for manipulation than historical cost data. Furthermore, data in operational accounting are under less severe rules and regulations than those in equity accounting. Therefore, the public would quickly discover that every firm attempted to paint a bright financial picture of the firm in the minds of the public in order to attach more investment to the firm under favorable terms and to raise the market price of its stock. The demand for the disclosure of financial statements based on historical costs would grow stronger and stronger since these types of statements are regulated by more rigorous rules and are far less subject to manipulation. The public would consider current cost data to be a good supplement to historical cost data but not a substitute.

I leave it to the reader to judge how long the practice of barring historical cost data could be continued in this hypothetical country.

Finally, I would like to point out that the issue of asset valuation is only one of the many issues that accountants should explore in developing an accounting system for society. I do not object to current cost accounting if one can show that its benefit to society is greater than its cost of implementation. Remember, however, the bill to society for establishing and running such a system can be enormous, considering the cost of assessment, calculation, and auditing (all of which must be done every year) as well as the cost of solving disputes if the firm or the accountants are challenged on the reliability of data or are accused of intending to mislead the public. (Financial statements under historical costs are prepared as a by-product of equity accounting, hence, insofar as equity accounting is considered to be indispensable, the additional cost of publishing financial statements is negligible relative to the cost incurred under current costs.)

I believe we should explore other ways of providing useful information to the investors instead of limiting our attention to valuation problems only. Let us explore such a possibility in Country E.

In Country E, historical cost accounting is recognized not only as the basis for equity accounting but also as an important source of data in operational accounting. Thus, historical cost data are made available to the management for their use in decision making. Also, financial statements based on a historical cost valuation are published for the public.

However, accountants in this country also realize that historical cost data are only a modest portion of data needed by the management and the public in making decisions on resource allocation. Unlike the accountants in Country D who attempted to improve the data of operational accounting by changing the valuation method, accountants in Country E try to expand the kinds of data they record and report.

For example, they have succeeded in establishing a recording and reporting system on the commitment basis.[4] This is an attempt to better control contracts and other financial commitments that management makes, and also to provide information in financial statements on outstanding sales, •purchases, construction contracts, etc. These

---

[4] See Yuji Ijiri, "On the Commitment Basis of Recording and Reporting Transactions," to be published in *The Proceedings of Scandinavian-GSIA Joint Faculty Seminar*, University of Göteborg, Sweden, 1971.

commitments are reasonably good indicators of how the financial situation of the firm is going to *actually* change, unlike data in current cost accounting which are derived from contemplated (replacement or disposal) transactions that the firm is almost certainly *not* going to undertake. The change to the commitment basis of accounting was initiated both to protect the equity of interested parties (equity accounting) by placing contracts and other financial commitments under the same control as regular resources and also to provide relevant data to the management and the public in making their decisions (operational accounting).

Another direction in which accountants in Country E are attempting to move is toward a more timely reporting system. They feel that reporting financial data annually is too infrequent to be of much use to the public in this day of computer technology. A committee was appointed whose members were selected from public accounting firms, industry, financial analysts, etc., to set up rules detailing the facts that must be immediately disclosed to the public and the conditions of their disclosure.

Efforts were made to specify the rules in such a way that they could be applied most objectively in determining the need for disclosure and the contents to be disclosed. Major events that were considered by the committee included mergers and acquisitions, construction of major plants, introduction of new product lines which would substantially change the product mix of the firm, major contracts and their cancellations, etc.

Rules for immediate public disclosure are very difficult to derive for two different reasons. One is that the interest of the management in protecting their trade secrets from disclosure to competitors and the public must be weighed against the investors' and the public's interest in timely information of major events of a firm. The second is concerned with a method for releasing the information to the public in the most equitable manner. When information dealt with by accountants was not so "hot," this was not a problem. But as accountants work with more and more crucial information to the investors, this second problem becomes more and more serious. The committee is still studying the rules for immediate public disclosure from these two angles.

I do not have the answers to these two difficult problems, but I am certain that these are the crucial problems we must face if we continue to make an effort to provide relevant data to investors for their investment decisions.

Although these difficulties with operational accounting exist for the investors and the public, operational accounting for management seems to hold no major barrier to unlimited progress. It appears that the most promising area in which accountants can concentrate their efforts is to develop integrated accounting and management information systems by coordinating their efforts with developments in the computers and systems area. The benefit to the investors and to society that can be derived from such efforts are indirect but certain.

### III. Conclusion

I shall summarize the arguments presented in the previous section in the following five propositions.

### Proposition 1

Historical cost valuation is the only valuation method which includes, as an integral part of its valuation procedure structured on the double-entry bookkeeping system, the essential requirement of equity accounting that every actual change in the resources of an entity be recorded by relating inputs and outputs so that it can be traced and identified whenever necessary.

### Proposition 2

Historical cost valuation provides data that are less disputable than data provided under other valuation methods currently being proposed, an essential requirement in equity accounting.

### Proposition 3

Historical cost valuation by refusing to recognize holding gains and losses, is in line with the spirit of maintaining the status quo unless changes (in income) are proved to be necessary beyond any reasonable doubt. This spirit is essential for solving conflicts of interest and maintaining order and stability in society.

*Proposition 4*

Historical cost valuation provides data that are useful for decision-making by insightful managers and investors insofar as history is the only basis for predicting the future.

*Proposition 5*

Historical cost valuation is among all valuation methods currently proposed, the method that is least costly to society, considering the social costs of recording, reporting, auditing, settling disputes, etc.

# Response to
# A Defense for Historical Cost Accounting

*by* JAMES H. MacNEILL
PEAT, MARWICK, MITCHELL & CO.
*on leave from* FORDHAM UNIVERSITY

PROFESSOR IJIRI does not consider historical cost to have all the answers and so we start on common ground. He does not completely reject alternatives to historical cost on the basis of utility or relevance. Instead, his argument is addressed to the difficulties and limitations of implementing alternatives.

For Country A, he has decreed that a single entry system is in force, but it is based on current valuations rather than historical cost. The lack of records showing resource flows is irrelevant to the current cost system only by his definition; it is actually most relevant to those who would use the system. Similarly, I think that control features are lacking, not because of anything that is inherent in current cost as a valuation method but simply by fiat of the country itself.

Now in Country B, the weakness in control that existed in Country A is partially overcome because Country B has records of changes kept in terms of physical units. As the British newscaster said when the Profumo scandal broke, this was the first *hetero*-sexual scandal in Britain in some time, and that was progress of a sort. So, Country B has progress of a sort.

Country C progresses a little further in that some historical records are kept. Although it is argued that there is a danger that income determination becomes a process of political negotiation rather than a process of systematic calculations, I submit that under present day accounting, political negotiations are involved in many areas—union wage agreements and mergers and acquisitions, price-setting in contracts

15

and rate making. All are to a large extent the result of political negotiations despite the use of historical costs, maybe because of it. Historical cost may be that unique transaction among transactions, as Professor Ijiri states, but it has not enabled us to avoid disputes.

Now in connection with Country C, the argument is brought up that under a current cost valuation system, $\Sigma A > A_1 + A_2 + \cdots + A_n$, that is, the whole is greater than the sum of the parts. This, I think, is not anything inherent in current cost accounting. The value of the going concern is most often greater than the sum of its parts. This non-additivity is a more serious problem under historical than under current cost. We may not reach the ideal with current cost, but I submit that we are closer to it than we are under historical cost. We know at least that the parts are a little closer to being usefully valued, even though the value of the whole is still greater than the sum of the parts. Professor Ijiri asks, if a contemplated transaction, which is what current costs must be based upon, will actually take place? But I ask, will a deferred historical cost result in future benefit? Uncertainty must not be a reason for rejecting a system. It has to be an accepted condition of any useful system.

Country D has made further progress; accountants here believe that historical costs are of no use for decision making purposes. The public must be rather confused in Country D, however, because a single income figure is presented at historical cost, while details are given in current cost. This is the country where government agents audit the historical cost and they are the only ones who see the details of historical costs.

Now in Country E again there is some progress, but in a different direction. Although current cost data are unfortunately eliminated, certain commitments are reported, viz., sales and purchase orders, construction contracts and that sort of thing. Current accounting practices are admittedly quite narrow in not providing these data within the informational system. A further innovation in Country E is that certain events are made public as they occur. Timeliness, of course, is always a virtue.

Professor Ijiri's propositions summarize his position. Proposition 1 is that historical cost valuation is the only valuation method which requires double entry structure. I submit that historical cost can also be employed in a single entry system, where there is no relating of inputs to outputs. Therefore, historical cost, of itself, does not require double entry structure. Conversely, current cost accounting can be implemented by employing a double entry structure. In this approach, inputs and outputs are not only related, they are even more sharply identified and defined because, 1) through restatement at current costs, inputs and outputs are measured in terms relevant to present decisions, and 2) the results of exchanges are separated from the results of value changes, that is, operating gains and losses are distinguished from holding gains and losses.

Proposition 2 is that historical cost valuation provides data that are less disputable than those of other valuation methods. Perhaps the only thing we cannot dispute is that historical costs are historical costs. Even here, estimates and judgments make them subject to dispute at any time after the expenditure date. Unamortized historical cost, cost of unsold product, and capitalized versus expensed historical cost all involve uncertainty. Perhaps historical cost is less disputable only because we have accepted certain traditions with respect to its application. We have dogmatized the process and given it legitimacy. It might have been otherwise.

One way in which historical cost is less disputable is that, while we may not know which measure is most equitable and useful when ownerships change, we do know that historical costs are inequitable in periods other than those of economic stability. We also know that they are irrelevant to many management decisions. Here, I am thinking in terms of sunk costs. Decisions are intrinsically involved with the future. The balance between the certainties of historical costs and the uncertainties of the future will vary, but there is always some element of uncertainty. One cannot rely on certainties of the past to judge the uncertainties of the future.

Proposition 3 is that historical cost valuation is in line with the spirit of maintaining the status quo and provides tools to deal with conflicts of interest thus maintaining order and stability in society. Conflicts of interest have not been avoided through historical cost. When ownership changes hands, the parties can rarely base their settlement on historical cost statements. And although tax relief has largely been implemented through historical cost modifications, the shortcoming of historical cost has been one of the prime forces in tax reform movements.

Proposition 4 is that history is the only basis for predicting the future. History is useful in predicting the future, but it is not the only basis. One must recognize that historical events occurred under conditions that were unique to that time, and future conditions must be reckoned with. The fact that the value, however defined, of an asset has changed since its acquisition *is* history. It just happens that under present accounting practices, the change in value is generally not *recorded* history.

Proposition 5 is that historical cost valuation is the method that is least costly to the society. That, I think, is debatable. This is a question of fact; it can only be resolved through implementing a dual valuation process under the same conditions and then comparing their cost. I ask, incidentally, how would one measure the comparative cost of the two processes? Historical cost? Replacement cost? Opportunity cost? Price-level adjusted cost? Specifically, in regard to the expense of recording and reporting, one would have to give it a trial. Present accounting and auditing that are not oriented to current cost, I think, would simply be modified. We are doing this in forecasting to some extent. Regarding the cost of settling disputes, this would increase only if the incidence of disputes were increased and this, I think, is again debatable. Maybe we would have fewer disputes.

Professor Ijiri has employed useful hyperbole to make his points, but his progression is broken when current costs are dropped completely, as in Country E. Granted, custodianship reporting is useful, even essential; control of resources is necessary to management decisions; history is relevant to prediction; a structured system, such as double-entry, is desirable; and contemplated transactions must be quantified with a minimum of bias. But granting all these, they can still be achieved, I believe, within an integrated system of historical cost recording and current cost modification.

# 2

# On Current Replacement Costs
# and Business Income

### by PHILIP W. BELL
UNIVERSITY OF CALIFORNIA, SANTA CRUZ

## I. Historic Costs versus Current Costs

THE issue of whether historic costs or current costs should be used in the measurement of business income has been discussed so widely, particularly in the literature of the last ten years, that both sides are probably tempted simply to fall back on the Disraeli principle of always ending an argument in which he could neither convince his protagonist nor his protagonist convince him with one word, an exasperated "Perhaps." Still, it seems worthwhile in terms of the overall aims of this symposium, as I understand them, to stress three points on the current cost side and then move on.

First, the use of current cost data, at least as Professor Edwards and I have employed them,[1] does *not* need to exclude historic cost data from accounting records. End-of-period adjustments are made to historic cost figures on the basis of current cost values, but *both* are then reported in somewhat rearranged form in finished accounting statements—nothing is lost and a great deal, we feel, is gained. The other two points I wish to stress, then, relate to what is thereby gained.

One very important improvement in the records of the enterprise is that the resultant data properly separate operating from holding

---

[1] Edgar O. Edwards and Philip W. Bell, *The Theory and Measurement of Business Income* (Berkeley, California: University of California Press, 1961).

19

gains of the firm, something that use of historic cost information clearly does not do.

The other, less widely recognized but equally important advantage of using current costs in developing accounting records for the firm is that by so doing, one can recognize in the accounts all gains of the enterprise *as they accrue, as well as* when they are realized. *Not* counting gains when they arise has the unfortunate consequence that when such gains are in fact realized, the gains earned over the full span of time during which the assets were held are attributed entirely to the period in which the gains are realized. This difficulty carries with it two implications: First, it means that even though absolutely identical events occur in two periods, accounting data will normally yield a different figure for profits reportedly earned in the two periods, because the data for each period are influenced by data of past periods. Second, if holding gains are only reported when realized through sale, there is no way to determine in what periods holding activities were successful and in what periods they were unsuccessful.

Before briefly illustrating these points, let me re-emphasize what I stressed at the outset: the use of current costs in accounting records in order to achieve the above advantages does not have to obviate employment of historic costs; indeed, the methods we employ build upon traditional accounting principles and keep track of historic costs both in daily internal records and in finished balance sheets and income statements. Surely no one can complain of more, rather than less, information when he can accumulate the additional information at very little time and cost, and when the additional information permits statements which have the above advantages, which statements he (and others) can use or not as they see fit.

At a risk of seeming to vastly oversimplify and exaggerate, let me give a brief, much truncated illustration of the above arguments. A small enterprise, the XYZ Corporation, earns sales revenues over a three-year period of $40,000, $50,000, and $60,000, respectively. Its costs include payment of wages and salaries, which rise slightly each year. Under present historic cost methods of accounting, it computes its materials costs in accordance with some generally accepted principle (such as FIFO or LIFO) which is related to a completely artificial assumption about physical movements of goods and which, if there are physical changes of inventory stocks as in the LIFO case, does not accurately reflect the current costs of materials used in production when there are price changes. Depreciation cost of machinery used is another cost: machinery is purchased at the beginning of operations in Year 1 for $80,000 and is to be depreciated on a straight-line basis over a ten-year period, no salvage value, at $8,000 per year. Similarly, we shall assume that land and building are depreciated over a twenty-year period on the same basis, having been acquired also for $80,000. These costs are subtracted from revenue each year, and the income which traditional accounting practices yield, as shown in Figure 1A, suggests that the enterprise is doing very well, with income rising from $7,000 to $15,000 to $21,500. With no additional outlay of capital, the data suggest that this might be a good enterprise to invest in, or expand investment in.

Revenues are going up for this enterprise, perhaps because of larger output, perhaps because of rising prices—let us assume that it is largely the latter and that prices of materials, machinery, land, and building are also rising, in this case at a more rapid rate than what is being sold. Actual data do show sharp differences in movements of prices of individual assets from those of the general wholesale price index, both in this country and abroad.[2] Specifically, for ease of illustration, let us assume in the case of machinery that, if purchased in the second year rather than the first it would cost $140,000, and $180,000 in the third year. Further assume that the replacement cost of land and buildings in Years 2 and 3 would have been $120,000 and $180,000, respectively. We also assume that the true current cost of materials used also differs somewhat from those arrived at by our artificial inventorying methods.

Using current costs of operation, rather than historic costs, our income statement would appear as in Figure 1B. The purchase price of machinery being used is, in Year 2, $140,000 rather than the original $80,000. The current cost of using it in that year is then $14,000 on a ten-year depreciation basis, not $8,000, and a similar adjustment must be made for the rising cost of land and buildings. With our three outdated cost items adjusted to the true current cost of using

---

[2] See, for example, Edwards and Bell, p. 20; D. H. Whitehead, "Price-Cutting and Wage Policy," *Economic Record*, No. 39 (June 1963), p. 189; W. A. H. Godley and C. Gillion, "Pricing Behavior in the Engineering Industry," *National Institute Economic Review*, No. 28 (May 1964), pp. 50–52.

**Figure 1A**

THREE-YEAR INCOME STATEMENT FOR ENTERPRISE XYZ
(TRADITIONAL HISTORIC COST ACCOUNTING METHODS)

|  | YEAR 1 | | YEAR 2 | YEAR 3 |
|---|---|---|---|---|
| REVENUE | | $40,000 | $50,000 | $60,000 |
| COST | | | | |
| WAGES & SALARIES | $14,000 | | $15,000 | $17,500 |
| MATERIALS | 7,000 | | 8,000 | 9,000 |
| DEPRECIATION, MACHINERY | 8,000 | | 8,000 | 8,000 |
| DEPRECIATION, LAND & BUILDING | 4,000 | | 4,000 | 4,000 |
| | | 33,000 | 35,000 | 38,500 |
| INCOME | | $ 7,000 | $15,000 | $21,500 |

those items (wages and salaries, like revenues, are presumably already based on current prices of the year in question), our income statements come out very differently than that shown with traditional accounting practices. Figure 1B shows that income on operations is actually *declining* year-by-year, rather than increasing nicely, as suggested by traditional accounting methods as shown in Figure 1A.

Now we have shown, of course, only part of what has actually been

**Figure 1B**

THREE-YEAR OPERATING INCOME STATEMENT FOR ENTERPRISE XYZ
(CURRENT COSTS MATCHED WITH CURRENT REVENUES)

|  | YEAR 1 | | YEAR 2 | YEAR 3 |
|---|---|---|---|---|
| REVENUE | | $40,000 | $50,000 | $60,000 |
| COST | | | | |
| WAGES & SALARIES | $14,000 | | $15,000 | $17,500 |
| MATERIALS | 7,000 | | 9,000 | 11,500 |
| DEPRECIATION, MACHINERY | 8,000 | | 14,000 | 18,000 |
| DEPRECIATION, LAND & BUILDING | 4,000 | | 6,000 | 9,000 |
| | | 33,000 | 44,000 | 55,000 |
| INCOME | | $ 7,000 | $ 6,000 | $ 5,000 |

taking place by utilizing current costs to measure operating gains or losses. The gently rising material costs and sharply rising fixed asset costs not only involve rising *operating costs*, when measured in terms of current prices to make them comparable to other items on the income statement, but also involve *holding gains*, or preferably we may term them *cost savings*. Given the assumption that machinery, new, rose in value suddenly at the beginning of Year 2 from $80,000 to $140,000, the difference between current cost depreciation and historic cost depreciation in Year 2 of $6,000 is a cost saving realized during the year, from using machinery purchased originally for $80,000 but now costing $140,000.[3] Looked at over a longer term, machinery which was worth $72,000 at the end of the first year ($80,000 less $8,000) and $112,000 at the end of the second year ($140,000 less $28,000) as well as use value during the second year of $14,000 would involve total realizable (realized and unrealized) cost savings of $54,000 at the end of Year 2, of which $6,000 was actually realized through use in the second year, and another $6,000 will be used up in each of its subsequent eight years of life if held to maturity and assuming no further price changes. In Year 2, we feel that *both the realized and unrealized cost savings* of that year should be reported, so that they can be distinguished separately, on the income statement for that year. This is done in Figure 2, having made similar adjustments necessary for items other than those of the machinery account.[4] Only if this is done will the two advantages from utilizing current cost data cited at the beginning of this section be incorporated in the accounts. Operating gains are correctly separated from realized holding gains on the left, although the *total* of realized income is the same as that reported using traditional historic costs. The *total earned income* on the right (realized and unrealized) is the amount, and the only amount, which will prove

[3] We have used abrupt price changes for this much simplified example, rather than measurement of income in terms of average prices for a period, a practice criticized by Professor Chambers. In Edwards and Bell, we try to show rigorously why we think that an averaging process is quite acceptable (see Chapters V and VI, particularly pp. 144–147, with respect to inventories). Russell Mathews has also tried to answer Professor Chambers' criticism, particularly with respect to consistency of income and balance sheet statements. See his, "The Price-Level Controversy: A Reply," *Journal of Accounting Research* (Spring 1967), pp. 116–118.

[4] How such adjustments are handled in practice in ledger account adjustments at the end of the year, providing consistency in income and balance sheet accounts, is detailed in Edwards and Bell, Chapters V and VI.

## Figure 2

YEAR 2 COMPREHENSIVE INCOME STATEMENT FOR ENTERPRISE XYZ

REVENUE  ................................................................................................................  $50,000

COSTS

| | | |
|---|---|---|
| WAGES & SALARIES  ........................................................ | $15,000 | |
| MATERIALS  ........................................................................ | 9,000 | |
| DEPRECIATION, MACHINERY  .......................... | 14,000 | |
| DEPRECIATION, LAND & BUILDINGS  ................ | 6,000 | |
| | | 44,000 |

CURRENT OPERATING INCOME  ........................................................  $ 6,000

---

| CURRENT OPERATING PROFIT  .............................. $ 6,000 | CURRENT OPERATING PROFIT  .............................. $ 6,000 |
|---|---|
| REALIZED COST SAVINGS ON COST OF MATERIALS ... $ 1,000 ON DEPRECIATION, MACHINERY .. 6,000 ON DEPRECIATION, LAND & BUILDINGS ... 2,000 _____ 9,000 | REALIZABLE COST SAVINGS ON INVENTORIES.. $ 500 ON MACHINERY .. 54,000 ON LAND & BUILDINGS ........ 38,000 _____ 92,500 |
| REALIZED INCOME ........... $15,000 | EARNED INCOME ........... $98,500 |

---

to be the same when identical events, with respect to operations and individual price changes, occur in the life of the enterprise.[5]

This is as much as we can say here about the historic cost-current cost controversy, for we must move on to other issues. We will touch on the feasibility of acquiring sound current cost data for income statements, such as that shown in Figure 2, at the end. Let us now turn to the problem of dealing with price-level changes. The use of a simple adjustment for general price-level changes, rather than for individual price changes—as suggested by many accountants—is an adjustment which can readily be tacked on to the current cost data which we have suggested. However, we can only honestly say, that such an adjustment is an aberration of the first magnitude if applied without introduction of current costs, i.e., if it is applied to simple historic cost data.

[5] For a particularly telling example of this, affecting LIFO inventory valuation methods, see Edwards and Bell, Table 7, p. 156, and explanation, p. 158.

## II. The Problem of Price-Level Changes

I gladly concede that it is a digression from the subject of this paper, and indeed from the general subject of this symposium, to discuss general *price-level* changes. But we are forced into the matter because of the well-known monograph published by the American Institute of Certified Public Accountants in 1963 entitled *Reporting the Financial Effects of Price-Level Changes*.[6] Though it was not the intention of the authors, I fear the effect of this monograph was to lead some accountants to believe that making a single price-level adjustment to historic cost data served to deal with changing prices in the economy and thus obviated the need for current cost adjustments, such as we have been proposing here. Nothing could be further from the case. Once meaningful data have been accumulated on operating income and holding gains, *then* a general price-level adjustment may be made in assets and liabilities on the balance sheet and a "real" income figure consistent with these values may be readily computed. Such an exercise adds relatively little to the usefulness of accounting data for decision-making by internal and external users, which we feel should be the primary concern of the accountant.[7] But unless cost figures are first adjusted to current values, i.e., account taken of *individual* price changes, one is left with "meaningless data," as R. L. Mathews put it in his, to my mind, excellent critique of the ARS 6.[8] "Data which are measured in different units to begin with cannot be converted to a common basis of measurement merely by applying a common conversion factor," Mathews correctly argues.[9] Indeed, because prices of individual assets may frequently move *opposite in direction* to a general consumer price index in the economy,[10] a general price-level adjustment to historic cost asset values may, in

---

[6] Staff of the Accounting Research Division, American Institute of Certified Public Accountants, *Reporting the Financial Effects of Price-Level Changes*. Accounting Research Study No. 6 (New York: American Institute of Certified Public Accountants, Inc., 1963).

[7] See Edwards and Bell, Chapter VIII, especially pp. 264–269.

[8] R. L. Mathews, "Price-Level Changes and Useless Information," *Journal of Accounting Research* (Spring 1965), pp. 133–155.

[9] *Ibid*, p. 147.

[10] As found by Whitehead, *op. cit.*, for Australia in 1954–58, for example, and as was true for electrical machinery vis-a-vis consumer prices in the United States between 1961 and 1966.

fact, move one *away from* rather *than toward* a true current cost income picture.

But, we would argue, the price-level adjustment approach to problems of income measurement is bleaker still. The utility of adjusting even meaningful income data for changes in the value of the dollar is really quite limited. Issues with respect to the payment of dividends and maintenance of real capital are, of course, the primary ones put forward for the importance of a proper measurement of real income. To the extent that management substitutes growth in real capital for profitability as a goal, the additional information would, of course, affect decisions, although such a goal would be difficult to rationalize, whether to owners, investors, or others interested in general economic decisions with respect to the allocation of resources in an economy. In fact, if fund retention is based on profit alternatives available to the firm, the identification of real profit should not alter the amount paid in dividends, even if real capital is impaired by payment. Even the "going concern" convention does not suggest that a concern must continue at a constant or expanding level of real capital if owners are thereby pushed into putting earned profits into what should, on economic grounds, be a declining business firm.

This is not to suggest that real income data are of negligible significance, for clearly, movements in the general price-level have a bearing on a firm's access to funds and on other considerations which may influence its total economic situation, including taxes paid on what may be thought of as fictional (as opposed to real) gains. (There is little doubt, in my mind at any rate, that the hope to lower corporate taxes has served as the primary impetus underlying the interest in adjusting business data, however compiled, for changes in the general price-level.) The fact of the matter is that comparisons among firms at a moment of time, and of trends in one firm over time serve as the primary valid reason for adjusting properly constructed income and balance sheet data for changes in the value of the dollar.

So much for corrections in accounting information for changes in the general price-level—adjustments which can readily be made to our current cost data if this is desired. We now turn to what we believe is a much more relevant and perhaps divisive issue at this conference—the question of how current costs are to be defined if they are to be used in accounts, or more specifically, the question of whether entry or replacement cost values are to be used (or exit or opportunity cost values) in measuring current costs.

### III.  *Entry (Replacement Cost) versus Exit (Opportunity Cost)*
### *Values in the Measurement of Current Costs*

In our book, we delineated eighteen different concepts which might be relevant to the valuation problem in accounting, based on past, current, or future entry and exit values on the one hand, and on the form of what was being valued (initial inputs, present form, or ultimate form) on the other, in one grand matrix, and I am sure that the matrix did not exhaust all the possibilities.[11] But here I wish to dwell on only two of those eighteen concepts or matrix entries: (1) the current entry or replacement costs of initial inputs versus (2) the current exit or opportunity costs of the present form of existing assets.

In thinking about the basic issue, I could not help but reflect on an experience I had in East Africa in 1963–64, when I served as one of three members of an Economy Commission for the University of East Africa—a commission designed to somehow cut $300,000 out of a 1.5 million dollar budget for a new federal University being designed for the countries of Kenya, Tanzania, and Uganda. At Makerere University in Uganda (the older, more experienced entity of the three being joined together, and indeed the pearl of the widespread University of London network in overseas colonies) we were given a budget for expenditures broken into various categories for 1961–62, 1962–63, and 1963–64. I asked if we might have the actual expenditures, using the same categories, for the years then past, and was told, "No, we do not have those." "But then how do you make up your budget for the succeeding year?" The answer came back, "On the basis of the budget of the preceding year." It turned out that actual expenditures were never compared with planned or budgeted expenditures in devising future plans!

The essence of my argument here is that first things must come first, and that the first task of any enterprise is to measure the profitability or performance of plans and decisions *which were actually made for some period ahead*, and thus evaluate performance against the expectations one originally had. Certain assets were purchased with a plan

---

[11] Edwards and Bell, p. 77.

of operations in mind. That plan, those operations, indeed those people who developed that plan, must first be evaluated before alternatives about the future can be considered, and it is the accountant's task to provide the data for that evaluation. Once this is done, *then* one can compare the cost of continuing to use the assets for the purposes for which they were originally acquired, as opposed to acquiring and using some other assets for these purposes (a measure involving use of the cost of best alternative services as a measure of current cost, as proposed by R. H. Parker and G. C. Harcourt,[12] and/or selling the assets and using the cash received for some other purpose, i.e., using opportunity cost as a measure of current cost as proposed by Chambers.[13] Let me make clear that both of these alternatives are relevant to the decision-making process. But a meaningful concept of profit, as we see it, is the measurement of performance in terms of what was originally intended. Only after this plan is evaluated can one proceed to the next stage of deciding whether or not performance should be changed.

In these terms, Professor Chambers' concept of profit, if we understand it correctly, would have to be that a business plan would always have to be one of maximizing the acquirable cash equivalent of assets over successive short-run periods. This would seem to be where using the exit value or opportunity cost value of assets, period-by-period, to compare with current revenues leads us. For a firm dealing with anything more than the simplest retail or wholesale trading operations, that is, for one involved in any kind of production, such a view of the enterprise, its objectives, and its mode of thought, would just not seem to be applicable.[14] Current user cost, or the current replacement cost of assets the firm has, in fact, chosen to employ in its plan of

---

[12] R. H. Parker and G. C. Harcourt, *Readings in the Concept and Measurement of Income* (Cambridge, England: Cambridge University Press, 1969), p. 19.

[13] For example, he writes: "The current cash equivalents of the assets of a going concern are the sums obtainable in the short-run in the ordinary course of business; that is, market resale prices in the short-run. The measure of the cost of using an asset is its then market resale price." See R. J. Chambers, *Accounting, Evaluation and Economic Behavior* (Englewood Cliffs, New Jersey: Prentice-Hall, 1966), p. 218.

[14] Professor Sterling, who also rejects entry for exit prices, would seem to be treating almost exclusively a rather simplified trading entity. See Robert R. Sterling, *Theory and Measurement of Enterprise Income* (Lawrence, Kansas: University Press of Kansas, 1970), especially pp. 328–330.

operation would, we suggest, be the relevant data to match against current revenues to measure the relative success or failure, i.e., performance of the enterprise, both for internal and external users of such accounting data. Therefore, current user cost would be the cost of primary concern to the accountant in carrying out his function for the firm and for the world at large. Once the performance has been measured, *then* the accountant, in conjunction with cost engineers, business planners, or what not, can go ahead and help to assess how to modify the existing or present plan of operation, or support the firm in adopting a new one.

While briefly put forward, that is really the essence of our argument for using entry, rather than exit, values as the proper measures of current costs, which we feel are so essential for accounting records. Under certain ideal conditions, there may exist no difference in the two measures of current cost, of course, but such ideal conditions, like most ideal conditions, never actually prevail in practice. The ideal conditions would be the following:

1. There must exist a large number of identical assets traded on one market so that market prices are known for both new and used assets;
2. The firm must have nondiscriminatory access to both the buying and selling sides of that market;
3. There must be no transportation or installation costs involved in either the purchase or the sale of the particular asset in question.

Now, such conditions rarely, if ever, exist in the real world, so we are talking about two different concepts of current cost here. David Solomons has treated this whole issue with considerable care,[15] and his argument for use of current replacement costs (entry values) rather than opportunity costs (exit values) has been very briefly but, we think, well summarized in the Parker-Harcourt volume.[16] What Parker and Harcourt show, following Solomons, is that current replacement cost (entry value) use, as opposed to opportunity cost (exit value) use, generally has more economic meaning to the firm under most circumstances. Replacement Cost (RC) is almost invariably the upper

[15] See David Solomons, "Economic and Accounting Concepts of Cost and Value," *Modern Accounting Theory*, ed. Morton Backer (Englewood Cliffs, New Jersey: Prentice-Hall, 1966).
[16] Parker and Harcourt, pp. 17–18.

limit to current cost, as opposed to Net Realizable Value (NRV) or
the Present Value (PV) of the expected net cash receipts from the
asset where this may differ from RC and NRV because of, perhaps,
the existence of Goodwill or for some other reason. Parker and Harcourt argue that there are six hypothetical possible relationships among
these three values of RC, NRV, and PV, viz.:

| | | | |
|---|---|---|---|
| 1. | NRV > PV > RC | 4. | PV > NRV > RC |
| 2. | NRV > RC > PV | 5. | RC > PV > NRV |
| 3. | PV > RC > NRV | 6. | RC > NRV > PV |

They then proceed to divide these cases into two groups according
to whether the asset should be held for use or resale as follows:

| *Use* | | *Resale* | |
|---|---|---|---|
| 3. | PV > RC > NRV | 1. | NRV > PV > RC |
| 4. | PV > NRV > RC | 2. | NRV > RC > PV |
| 5. | RC > PV > NRV | 6. | RC > NRV > PV |

Deducting all NRV's from the "use" group as irrelevant and all PV's
from the "resale" group as irrelevant, and also remembering that the
upper limit of value to the firm is RC, the six cases can be written
as follows:

| *Use* | | *Resale* | |
|---|---|---|---|
| 3. | RC | 1. | RC |
| 4. | RC | 2. | RC |
| 5. | RC > PV | 6. | RC > NRV |

The final rule which arises from this little exercise is that the value
of an asset to the firm = RC, except where RC > PV or RC > NRV,
where value to the firm = PV or NRV, whichever is greater.

But, we would argue for current replacement cost as opposed to
opportunity cost on simpler grounds related to measuring performance
cited earlier rather than on the above, rather sophisticated theoretical
argument. Accounting must measure past events, and to be useful, it
must measure those which actually happened, not those which might
happen if a firm does something other than that which was planned.
As we have said, measure what has actually happened, then compare
with what might happen now or in the future. It is really on this
basis that our case for entry values rests, and we shall leave it at that
and see what the discussion brings out.

## IV. Flexibility, Feasibility, Complexity and Reliability:
## A Summing Up

We have tried to present a flexible plan for the measurement of the income of an enterprise—one which loses nothing in terms of present practices but adds a great deal. A key stumbling block to its acceptance in the profession would seem to be what we regard as mistaken notions as to its *feasibility*, its *complexity*, and its *reliability*. Let us treat the first two issues together.

We know of two examples where the Edwards-Bell data have been formulated in their entirety, i.e., involving many more adjustments than suggested in our grossly oversimplified example used for this paper, for business enterprises over several years time. In both cases, the results on operating profit, and of course on earned income, differed significantly from those arrived at by using traditional historic cost data, even though the works concentrated on operations in the early 1960's, which was a period of relatively mild price changes compared with the period of 1965-69.

Peter Dickerson, in a monograph published by the Institute of Business and Economic Research,[17] revised comprehensively the data for a "small producer of moulded plastic articles located on the West Coast," in operation only since 1956. He found for this *new firm* (wherein differences would not be expected to be as large as in older firms) that over a seven-year period (late 1950's and early 1960's) and a five-year period (1963-1968), when the consumer price index rose 11 percent and 14 percent, respectively, the use of current costs actually *raised* current operating income from $82,000 to $94,000, or slightly under 15 percent, whereas a general price-level adjustment of historic costs would have *reduced* the figure to $78,000. What is *more important* in many ways to the misunderstood issue of complexity, however, is that in adjusting the whole array of data for this firm to conform to that shown in Figure 2 above (except that the number of items to be adjusted were enormously more intricate and complex, with the computations very carefully done and with income and balance sheets produced in both "money" and "real" terms for the seven-year period) Mr. Dickerson reported that he spent a total time of only *95 hours of work* on the data, *40* of which were spent examining and

[17] Peter J. Dickerson, *Business Income—A Critical Analysis*, Institute of Business and Economic Research (Berkeley: University of California Press, 1965).

analyzing the enterprise's books, i.e., getting used to them. What may seem to be quite difficult and complex at first blush is really not so at all, we feel, once the system is understood. Yet, as indicated, much more realistic and relevant data are supplied to internal and external users.

The other attempt to employ the Edwards-Bell approach reported in available (in this case, unpublished) literature that I am aware of was done here in Kansas by Robert Hollinger of Kansas State University. The application was to a wholesaling firm only over a three-year period (1964–66, also a period of relative price stability). Over this period, the rise in income in accordance with the conventional accounting practices involving use of historic costs was $1,845,000, or 72 percent, whereas true operating income, in our sense, rose only by $440,000, or 16 percent. The residual or difference between these two figures, of course, actually involved holding gains rather than operating gains—gains which might be expected to be especially significant for a wholesaling firm.

We turn, finally, to the last issue which bothers many accountants a great deal, that of feasibility. Current cost figures on inventories are relatively easy to arrive at, but what about fixed assets—can current data on them be arrived at in reliable fashion? For those accountants hopelessly wedded to that "sacred cow" of accounting—the "objectivity principle"—perhaps not. Certainly, there are now available a wide range of official Government indices on fixed asset prices of various kinds, and there is always the possibility of appraisals and/or checking back with suppliers. But our principal answer to those who we think worry excessively about "objectivity" and not enough about "realism and relevance" is that one can hardly help but come *closer* to good, meaningful data through use of current as opposed to historic cost. If a system is feasible, reasonably simple, and very likely to be much more relevant and useful for decision-making by both insiders and outsiders, why not adopt it?

# Response to
# On Current Replacement Costs
# and Business Income

*by* GEORGE R. CATLETT

ARTHUR ANDERSEN & CO.

I APPRECIATE the opportunity to participate in this symposium. Those of us in practice should occasionally stop our daily struggles with difficult problems and sit down with a group like this to discuss basic concepts and theories. The real question all of us face today is —what best presents the facts to the users of financial statements? Professor Bell's ideas are certainly something for us to think about. What he proposes is one approach to the problem of valuation, and I am inclined to agree with him that "economic realism" is very important, and that we do not give adequate attention to it in financial statements.

With inflation and with rapidly changing values, historical cost in financial statements, at least in some areas, is just not presenting the facts well enough, and we need to recognize that deficiency. The answers to the questions before us should not, in my view, be based primarily on matters such as feasibility, complexity and reliability. We need to find a way to do what really needs to be done. Professor Bell also mentions the sacred cow of objectivity. Certainly, we cannot forget objectivity and factors of that sort, but we may have paid too much attention to them. I sometimes think that there may be too many auditors on the Accounting Principles Board. Whenever a problem comes before the Board and a solution is suggested, you can see all of the auditors starting to worry about how difficult it will be to audit.

In many areas, of course, historical cost is the easiest thing to audit.

Also, historical cost is the easiest for a company to maintain in its records. And, with life being full of problems anyhow, why create more? Thus, there are pressures to retain historical cost in areas where it should not be retained. There are pressures to retain the cost basis from organizations such as the SEC. There are people at the SEC who can remember the 1920's and early '30's and are horrified at the thought of writing up assets for any purpose, or of doing anything which seems to be an upward adjustment. The SEC sent word to the Accounting Principles Board that it would prefer not to have any statement issued on price-level accounting. Everyone knows very well that price-level accounting does not represent a write-up, but the SEC does not like the appearance of an asset write-up; and so word was sent that the Board should forget the whole thing. Perhaps, at that time no one in the Federal Government wanted to admit that inflation existed. The Board was determined to issue the statement on price-level accounting anyhow, and it proceeded to do so. I might also add that in prospectuses, the SEC seldom lets a company even put in supplementary value information of any kind.

The cost of doing what needs to be done should not be a particular factor, if it is worth doing. Consideration should be given to the fact that listed securities today are worth hundreds of billions of dollars and there are 30 million stockholders; also, many billions of dollars are being loaned on the basis of financial statements, and there are numerous other uses to which financial statements are being put today. The difficulty and cost of doing more should have nothing to do with it whatsoever. The questions really are—what is the best thing to do and how do we accomplish the best presentation of the facts?

We are living in a difficult world and everything is more complex. As an example, calculations of earnings per share are now a major undertaking in some cases. When I started out in public accounting, earnings per share could be computed for a client in about a minute. Today, we have clients for whom it takes from several hours to several days to compute all of the different earnings per share. This is not the fault of the accounting profession. Companies have issued very complex and sophisticated types of securities, and we have to deal with them as they exist.

I have felt for some time that the accounting profession must face up to certain questions, both in asset valuation and in income realization.

Some of our ideas are going to have to be changed in both areas, and these matters are at the heart of many of the accounting problems with which we are now struggling. In fact, most subjects that come up in the Accounting Principles Board involve questions of asset valuation or income realization, and most of the problems in our daily practice revolve around these same questions. In the area of income realization, many of our concepts and rules are completely outmoded, but we keep on following them because of custom and the difficulty of making changes.

We could sit here today and perhaps determine what would appear to be a good system, but if we never could get it into effect, our discussion would not do much good. Any changes that are going to be made will be on an evolutionary, step-by-step basis. We know this is true because progress in practice cannot be made on any other basis. With the manner in which our society operates and all of the circumstances and forces which exist, improvements will occur by evolution. The question is—who will take the lead on an authoritative basis to see that the progress is in the right direction?

Nobody—the Accounting Principles Board, the SEC or anyone else—is going to figure out some new system of accounting for all of industry and put it into effect tomorrow morning. This cannot be done and will not be done. This does not mean that we should not establish what we want to do. The best of the alternatives should be selected and progress will then be achieved on a step-by-step basis.

One of the most frustrating aspects of working in this area in our firm and in the Accounting Principles Board is the difficulty of step-by-step evolution, which is involved in moving from historical cost to current cost or current value in some of these areas. In fact, the Board is trying to take a few little steps right now. At every turn we run into the argument that you cannot take this step because it is inconsistent with 22 others. Everybody knows that everything is not going to be changed at once. So, nothing is done. George O. May talked about this point in an article he wrote many years ago when the Committee on Accounting Procedure was in its early stages. He also indicated that everything cannot be changed at once, and that this fact becomes a roadblock to changing anything.

Take as an example, the area of marketable securities. I do not see any reason why marketable securities, if they are really marketable and can be sold in ten seconds by picking up the telephone, should not be carried at market value. This seems obvious, and the Board may some time try to take that step. However, you would be amazed how many people say: "Oh, you cannot do that because there are many other assets that are not carried at fair value or current value, and you cannot change this unless you change those." Therefore, we do not even take the first step. There are great pressures against each of these first steps. Sometimes people honestly believe that all of this must constantly be consistent (even though we already have many alternative practices and other inconsistencies); and at other times, their attitudes seem to be just defensive, because they know that all of the changes are not going to be made at once.

There is no question in my mind that right now we are in the process of moving toward current-value accounting. There are several subjects in this area on the Board's agenda now—marketable securities; basis for carrying long-term investments in common stock of other companies which are not subsidiaries; and, of course, the pooling, purchase and goodwill matter. These subjects, which are coming up, are being faced on a piecemeal basis. The difficulty that we are facing and the problems we are having in trying to deal with them are not so much that we are trying to do it on a step-by-step basis, which is the only way we will ever do it anyhow, but that no one has worked out any overall plan or system into which the solutions can be fit. No one on the Accounting Principles Board and no one in the whole decision-making area has ever really figured out what the purposes and objectives of financial statements are on an overall basis. When you stop and think about this for a minute, you realize that this is the only way to achieve progress—to figure out where we are going; devise an integrated plan; and fit the pieces in. Then, when people say, "You cannot take one step because other things are not being changed," the answer is that when all steps are taken, they will all fit together as a part of an overall plan. We do this today, we do that tomorrow, and we do something else the next day—and when all is done, a complete and integrated picture will be painted. People can understand that, but if you do not have a plan or system or objectives, then the results will not fit together. In fact, they will never fit together, and all you have is a bunch of isolated answers that end up being terribly inconsistent and uncoordinated.

Professor Bell states in his paper that the use of current costs permits us to "recognize in the accounts all gains of the enterprise *as they accrue, as well as* when they are realized." (p. 20) This statement is based on the assumption that such gains are in fact accruing. The critical issues are: (1) what constitutes income, and (2) when should such income be recognized?

I would not defend historical cost as the best basis for accounting in all areas. There is no question that current or fair values in one form or another may frequently be more useful information. The trend, even though painfully slow, is toward some form of current-value accounting because of the increasing disparity between historical cost and current value. This disparity is due, in part, to inflation, but certainly not entirely so. I have thought for some time that current-value accounting may be accepted in the United States before price-level accounting because the former is much easier to understand. The alleged advantage of price level accounting is that it is based on a mechanical computation which can be easily verified.[1] However, the ease of computation is not matched by the ease of understanding and comprehension.

I agree with Professor Bell that price-level accounting based on a general purchasing-power index does not have any relationship to current costs, or with current values. Of course, price-level accounting does not purport to have any such relationship.

I would also agree that accounting has not adequately reflected the passage of time, and this may be one of its greatest deficiencies. Time is a tremendous factor in the operation of a business and in business decisions. Yet, in many respects it is ignored in accounting. As a simple example, oil reserves may be purchased with an estimated production period of 15 years. At present interest rates, very little is

---

[1] "If this conjecture is true—that accounting is viewed as a calculational process with the factors supplied by somebody else—it would partially explain why some suggestions have become accepted accounting practices and others have not. It would also permit some predictions as to which suggestions will become accepted and which will not. For example, price-level adjusted historical costs will become an accepted accounting practice because one can calculate those figures and the index used for the calculation is supplied by somebody else. Non-cost valuation proposals will not become accepted accounting practices because one cannot normally calculate replacement costs or current cash equivalents." Robert R. Sterling, "A Test of the Uniformity Hypothesis," *Abacus*, V, (September 1969), p. 47.

really paid for the production 12 to 15 years later. Yet, the cost depletion is the same for the last barrel as for the first barrel.

The process of income accrual and realization is one of our major problems. Considerable stress is placed upon words when it is said that income *accrues* at one time and is *realized* at another time, and that both of them may be different than *earned* income. This seems to represent degrees of income, which raises some questions in my mind. Under the percentage-of-completion method for contract accounting is income being accrued, realized or earned? When does income of any kind arise? Many problems have occurred in accounting for the sale of franchises and in accounting for land development companies, and questions of income accrual and realization are involved.

Let us look at a few examples of the type of area where we can be accused of missing the boat with historical cost accounting. Of course, it is particularly evident in the natural resource industries. If an oil company drills a well for $100,000, and a million dollars' worth of oil is discovered, and a qualified geologist determines that the million dollars is a reasonable estimate, it is a little silly to say that a $100,000 asset in that balance sheet is a fair presentation of that asset. This defies logic and reason, and can be considered misleading, because a million dollar asset is carried at $100,000. From an economic standpoint, does income arise when the oil is discovered or when the oil is produced?

A company with a vast quantity of timber land that was acquired in the early 1900's has a large amount of unrecorded and unrealized income. The net income of this company represents nothing but appreciation in the value of timber. If the company had to pay anywhere near the fair value of that timber, it might have an operating loss, and yet it is showing a big profit and people are paying a lot of money for its earning power. You begin to wonder who is fooling whom. In fact, the management sort of knows this, but may not even do it right in their own internal accounting. So, in the whole natural resource area, we are putting our head in the sand and issuing statements to the public which are, at best, somewhat misleading. Managements many times are fooling themselves, even though they know better, but they are using the same statements that other people are using. A management will tend to operate on the same accounting basis that its stockholders are looking at, because that is what they are judged by and not by something else.

There is the whole area of marketable securities which I mentioned earlier. If you have a $100,000 cost for marketable securities of General Motors or Du Pont and you could pick up the telephone and sell them for $200,000, how can this be completely ignored in the accounting? This is following old conventions without any reason. Of course, market values can go down as well as up, as evidenced by developments in recent months, but however they go, that is where they go, and that is what the facts are.

In the area of machinery and equipment, there are some different factors. Professor Bell in his paper discusses an example where the cost of machinery went from $80,000 to $140,000, an increase of $60,000 in one year, to illustrate his point. This is somewhat different than the marketable securities or the oil in the ground. With machinery, there are not only inflationary effects and rising costs but also technological improvements, as well as possible questions of recoverability. If the company had to pay $140,000 for that machinery, they might not have purchased it. So, other factors do enter into productive items such as machinery.

Now, let me mention briefly one type of problem we are facing every day, and you can try to fit in Professor Bell's approach and see how you would deal with it. All of us here who are in practice today would agree that one of the most difficult problems is the question of when income is realized. This has been true in the whole area of franchising, which has received extensive publicity. Some companies went big and fell hard; and there were serious problems involving the sale of franchises and when income really was earned, accrued, realized or whatever name you want to put on it. In retrospect, there is no doubt that some of these companies were picking up income that they really never had.

I had a problem a few days ago which I will mention briefly. There is a land development company in Florida. It buys raw land, and in this case, the land is sold in a raw state under a contract payable over a period, perhaps ten years, with an undertaking to develop the land up to a certain point within that period of time. In the sales dollar, there is 10 percent raw land cost, 30 percent development costs, and 40 percent sales and administrative costs, which leaves 20 percent profit. The company wants to record the sale when the contract is signed and pick up the entire profit. A reserve would be set up for future development and other costs. The company contends that the sales effort is the big item, and that the entire profit should be recognized at the time the sale is made. In addition, the contract carries a six percent interest rate, which is substantially lower than the going rate for this type of obligation. There are two questions. One is whether income should be recognized prior to the development work. The other is recording the six percent obligation at face amount—if those obligations were sold to anybody else, they would only bring about sixty cents on the dollar, because nobody is going to pay the face amount for six percent land development obligations in Florida. When is the income earned? What do you think?

As you know, more and more companies in the last ten years have made long-term investments in the common stock of other companies, which represent less than 50% of such stock outstanding. There have been many corporate joint ventures started, with three or four companies going together and starting a business in oil, mining, construction, chemicals, etc. In many of these cases, the companies in which the investment is made are paying out little if any dividends, because of the development-type situations. An investor company may have a 30% investment in a very successful joint venture, but the joint venture is not paying dividends for business reasons and the investor company may be paying a million dollars a year to carry the investment. Even though the investor company's share of the earnings may be two million dollars, our accounting rules say that the company should report a million dollar loss a year on the investment. This defies common sense and economic facts and is not only inadequate reporting but also misleading information. The Accounting Principles Board presently has this problem under consideration. The recognition of this equity in current earnings is not current-value accounting; and it could be viewed as adjusted cost.

Businessmen and the users of financial statements do not care about the details of our rules so long as they produce sensible results, but some of the rules make no sense under current conditions. It is no defense to merely say that we have always done it that way. The need for change is pressing in on us.

What is probably going to happen is that we are going to have a mixture of historical cost, price-level accounting, adjusted cost, and current-value accounting of some kind, and we will go through a period of this mixture depending on what kind makes the most sense in the particular areas. But, it is essential that we have our eye on where we are going and what we think would be the best in the end. Then, we fit each step into a plan instead of flying off in all directions at once. In other words, we should determine where we are trying to go before we decide how to get there.

# 3

# The Relevance of Evidence of Cash Flows

*by* George J. Staubus

UNIVERSITY OF KANSAS

*on leave from* UNIVERSITY OF CALIFORNIA, BERKELEY

THIS paper deals with the relevance, to investors and managers, of several measures of assets that utilize various types of evidence of future cash flows. Net realizable value, discounted future cash flows, replacement costs and historical cost are examples of the measures with which we shall concern ourselves. The most familiar types of evidence considered are contracts, market prices and "physical observation." In the interest of efficiency, the background material is presented in the form of the following series of premises:

I. The proper objective of accounting is to provide quantitative economic information to assist decision makers. This objective can be met more satisfactorily if accountants explicitly recognize the major users of accounting data and familiarize themselves with users' problems.

II. We recognize entity personnel and external investors as the primary users of the data accumulated in an entity's accounting system—for the purposes of this discussion.

III. Managers and other entity personnel use the products of the double entry system in making many decisions. Benefits and costs associated with limited categories of activities are of particular importance to managers.

42

IV. Investors do not have sources of information about amounts of net asset items that are superior to a balance sheet. They rely upon balance sheets for information as to the current amounts of net asset items and upon income statements for explanations of the changes in net assets from operations.

V. The future of accounting depends upon its ability to produce information that is worth more than it costs. The following framework may help accountants judge the net value of a proposed accounting procedure:

A. Determinants of gross value

   1. Relevance of the measure employed to the decisions to be made by users

   2. Reliability of the specific measurement

      a. Lack of dispersion

      b. Lack of displacement

      c. Comparability of components of a flow measure

   3. Effectiveness of communication

      a. Comparability (contextual reliability)

         i. Intertemporal

         ii. Intracompany

         iii. Intercompany

      b. Understandability

      c. Timeliness

         i. Frequency

         ii. Lag

      d. Optimal disclosure

         i. Sufficient detail—all material items

         ii. Not excessive

      e. Good format: headings, classifications, net figures, juxtaposition

B. Cost of providing information

VI. Accountants should find, select, accumulate and report evidence of valuations made by others.

### *I. Relevance*

The primary criterion of the usefulness of measures of financial properties is their *relevance* to *decisions*. *A financial property is relevant to a decision if, given sufficient materiality, it has the power to affect the decision.* In the economic order quantity decision model, $EOQ = \sqrt{2AP/S}$, S is the total cost of holding a unit of the commodity for a year. Any component of this total, and the total itself, is relevant to the EOQ decision if the decision-maker uses this model. An economic property may be considered *directly relevant* to a decision if a perfect measurement of that property would fill the specific need perfectly, i.e., as well as we could possibly desire. This does not mean that a reliable measurement of a relevant property is the only information needed about one alternative, but it does provide perfect information about one variable in the decision model. Unfortunately, reliable measurements of perfectly relevant properties are rarely available.

A property that is closely related to a relevant property may serve as a *surrogate* for a relevant property and may be said to be *indirectly relevant* to a decision. In the EOQ model, future holding costs are directly relevant; past holding costs are likely to be indirectly relevant because they are closely related to future costs.

Several typical qualities of relevance can be identified. A measure or property may lack any one of these qualities and, thereby, fail to qualify as a directly relevant property or measure. The crucial quality is *activity relevance*, meaning that the measure must reflect an activity that is of concern to the decision-maker. S in the EOQ model must reflect the costs of holding the commodity over time; receiving and issuing costs are not relevant at this point. To take another example, the external investor relies upon financial statements to help him predict aspects of the firm's future activities, e.g., earnings and dividends; the property of assets that he needs to know must have some relation to what will happen to the asset; the asset's past itinerary or a future course it could—but will not—take are activities that are not directly relevant to the investor's decision. His alternatives are to buy, not buy, sell or hold the firm's security; the company's financial statements must help him see what his returns will be if he buys or holds, not whether the firm should sell or hold a specific asset.[1] An accountant would be guilty of reporting an irrelevant asset amount if he were to show to investors nothing but the scrap value of a two-year-old ship if he found no evidence of early scrapping.

For a measure to be relevant to the managerial decision of holding an asset "as is" or disposing of it either by use or sale, it must tell the manager either the net advantages to be enjoyed by holding (and sacrificed by disposition) or the net advantages to be enjoyed by disposition (and sacrificed by holding). The manager needs to know both to make the decision; he will be fortunate if his accounting staff can help him with either. The accountant may be able to justify reporting (to the manager) the net realizable value of the asset, because it is a close surrogate for the cash flow to be enjoyed by disposition without further processing and it is relevant to the activity of selling the asset. The manager should compare it with the cash flow to be enjoyed by retaining the asset, if he can obtain this information.

When the managerial decision to be made is whether or not to do something that requires the use of an existing asset, such as using raw materials or plant assets in production, the advantages and disadvantages may be outlined as follows:

Advantage—the net realizable value of the resulting product, i.e., the gross value less other costs.

Disadvantage—the sacrifice resulting from using the asset in question. If we are to calculate this sacrifice, we must know the consequences of using the asset. What undesirable event will occur, or what desirable event will not occur, because the asset is used in production? Putting it another way, what will be the supply adjustment? Where will the incremental consumption of the asset "come from"? Exhibit I illustrates the possibilities.

We believe that the most common method of adjusting the supply of assets that is typically used internally is by changing future

---

[1] Occasionally an investor does have the opportunity to play a role in a decision regarding the sale or retention of firm assets, but we classify such a role as a managerial activity. Owner-managers, including stockholder-directors, need information that will help them make sell-or-hold decisions about entity assets but the typical stockholder, or bondholder, in a publicly held corporation is more concerned with sell-or-hold decisions for his security, and this requires knowledge of what is most likely to happen to the firm's assets.

## Exhibit I

### RELATIONSHIPS BETWEEN POSSIBLE SUPPLY ADJUSTMENTS AND COST OF USING AN ASSET

| Supply Adjustment | Financial Consequence | Possible Reliable Surrogate |
|---|---|---|
| **I.** Reduce another use of the asset. | | |
| A. An internal use, e.g., in a second product. | Loss of value in second use. | ? |
| B. An external use, i.e., sale. | Loss of future net realizable value. | Present net realizable value. |
| **II.** Increase future acquisitions of assets of the same type. | | |
| A. Acquisition by production. | Future production cost. | Current production cost. |
| B. Acquisition by purchase. | Future purchase cost. | Current purchase cost. |

production or purchase schedules for such assets. If so, the most common financial consequence of using more of an asset is adding to future acquisition costs; so future acquisition cost has activity relevance. Present replacement cost may be the best reliable surrogate for future acquisition cost. If, on the other hand, using more of the asset will result in selling less, then net realizable value by sale has activity relevance to the decision regarding use. Similarly, if using more for one product means robbing another production process, the value of the asset for use in the other production process has activity relevance.

*Entity relevance* requires that the measure be related to the entity whose asset is being measured. If we need replacement cost, we must find the price in the market in which this entity buys and add fringe costs that must be paid by this entity. If net realizable value is needed, we must refer to the market in which this entity sells. Estimates of asset lives must relate to the environment of the owner.

*Place relevance* requires that the measure take into consideration the location of the asset. Transportation costs between the place of a market quotation and the physical location of an asset must be considered in obtaining net realizable value, replacement cost or historical cost.

*Time relevance* requires that a measure reflect the existence of the property at the time the action being considered by the decision-maker will take place. Measures reflecting service potential at a time earlier than the present are rarely directly relevant, because decisions cannot be made in the past; future service potential is more commonly needed.

These qualities of relevance are related to the traditionally recognized ways of creating utility. Activity relevance reflects functional utility based on the form of a good. Entity relevance is related to possession utility; a good may have different values in the hands of different owners. Place relevance is necessary because transportation may create utility. Time relevance takes into consideration the effect of time on the utility of a good; holding may create or destroy utility.

One other quality of relevance should be noted here. *Completeness* is necessary for any specified measure to be of maximum usefulness. This requires that no material item of cost be omitted in a measure of cost; that the net part of net realizable value not be overlooked; that the probability of collection be considered in stating future cash inflows.

All of these qualities of relevance must be present if a measure is to be directly relevant to a decision. Omission of any one quality, however, does not necessarily make the measure completely irrelevant or useless, but it does make it indirectly, or imperfectly, relevant. Whether it is still useful depends upon its degree of correspondence with the perfectly relevant measure, the extent to which it meets other criteria of valuable information and upon the availability of alternative measures.[2]

Relevance is the primary criterion of valuable accounting data. In the next section, we appraise common asset measurement methods using the relevance criterion. To place that discussion in the proper setting, the reader should remember that while reliability, effectiveness of communication and cost of accounting are additional criteria

---

[2] The absence of one of these features of relevance may have a tendency to produce a bias in the measure in question. For example, omission of fringe costs may result in a routine understatement of costs or use of old prices may result in understatement in a period of rising prices. If this type of procedural bias is measurable, the decision-maker may be able to adjust for it and minimize the harmful consequences.

to be met by any accounting procedure that is adopted, the present paper focuses on relevance.

## II. The Relevance of Cash Flows

**We hypothesize that the property of an asset or a liability that is most frequently relevant to the decisions for which accounting data are helpful is the difference in the present value of the firm's future cash flows that will result from the existence of the asset or liability.** We do not intend to prove this hypothesis at this point, but we do feel obligated to provide enough support to assure its credibility.

First, let us consider the needs of *securities investors*. At least since Irving Fisher wrote, in 1906, that "the value of any capital-good, either of wealth or of property-rights, assuming that all future income is foreknown, is the discounted value of that income,"[3] the present value concept of securities values has been recognized by students of finance.[4] We believe that this view is now generally accepted among finance theorists. "The fundamental proposition of capital theory is that the value of an asset is the future payments it provides discounted at the appropriate rate."[5] More recently, the work of the American Accounting Association's Committee on External Reporting suggests that not only is the present value view of securities widely accepted but its implications for investors' interest in the firm's future cash flows can no longer be avoided. The Committee's dividend prediction model emphasized the firm's future cash flows from continued operations and from changes in its asset and liability positions to the virtual exclusion of all other attributes of net assets.[6] This work provides welcome support for a view that we have held for some fifteen years: the present value of the future cash flows resulting from the presence of an asset or liability is the property that is most *relevant* to securities investment decisions.

[3] Irving Fisher, *The Nature of Capital and Income* (New York: The Macmillan Company, 1906), p. 223.

[4] See Robert F. Wiese, "Investing for True Values," *Barron's*, September 8, 1930 and John Burr Williams, *The Theory of Investment Value* (Cambridge, Massachusetts: Harvard University Press, 1938), p. 6.

[5] Myron Gordon, *The Investment, Financing and Valuation of the Corporation* (Homewood, Illinois: Richard D. Irwin, Inc., 1962), p. 3.

[6] American Accounting Association, "An Evaluation of External Reporting Practices—A Report of the 1966–68 Committee on External Reporting," *The Accounting Review*, Supplement to XLIV (1969), pp. 79–123.

One of the major concerns of *managers* in most entities is to satisfy their employers, the owners (if the managers are not themselves the owners). Their measure of success is the same as owners'. In current jargon, the firm's objective function is generally recognized as maximizing either its present value or its market value. A measure of success, other than the change in the market value of the firm's securities, must be closely related to a measurement of a change in the present value of the firm over time. This requires the measurement of the firm's present value at two points in time which, in turn, requires the measurement of the various components of the firm's present value—assets and liabilities—if accounting is to have a role in it at all.

The broad spectrum of *management decisions*, surely, is as important a use of accounting data as any. Decisions that require information as to asset amounts generally involve possible changes from present plans; the alternative courses of action include at least (a) no change from present plans and (b) an alternative "use" or future course for the asset. The possible alternatives encompassed in (b) are, of course, numerous. Some of them are immediate sale of the asset (1) for scrap or (2) for a more typical use of the asset, leasing the asset to another party, switching it to a different use in its present location and changing both its use and its location within the firm. It is obvious that the accountant would have a hard time trying to provide asset amounts relevant to these alternatives as a matter of routine reporting. But, what is more important, the presently planned use is more likely to be an alternative in any managerial decision than is any single alternative use, so it is more likely to have *activity relevance* for managers.

This is a good time to remind ourselves of the role of present values of future cash flows in the analysis of capital investment opportunities. "Capital budgeting" models typically focus on the objective of investing in projects with positive net present values. If the decision is made primarily on the basis of an anticipated rate of return in excess of the cost of capital, the projects that are accepted have positive net present values. If the analysis focuses directly on the net present value of future cash flows discounted at the cost of capital rate, again projects with net present values are accepted. Finding and investing in projects with net present values is the logical managerial approach to specific asset purchase decisions and to maximizing the present value of the firm.

This section can now be summarized by saying that the present value of future cash flows resulting from assets and liabilities is the property that is most frequently relevant to financial decisions. The present value of future cash flows is the essence of securities values, the property of existing assets and liabilities that is most commonly relevant to the decisions of external investors and managers, and is the objective of the search for investment projects. In other words, the present value view of assets and liabilities is consistent with the most widely accepted ex ante approach to assets and with the generally accepted view of securities value. Accordingly, *we believe that the most useful meaning of asset and liability quantities is the item's incremental effect upon the net discounted amount of the entity's future cash flows.* This is what we seek to measure.

### III. Measures of Asset Amounts

Having defined the amount of an asset or liability as its incremental effect upon the net discounted amount of the firm's future cash flows, we must now turn to the implementation of this concept. How can we ascertain the amount of an asset or a liability? Accountants do not rely heavily on their own opinions of asset values, but they do rely upon their own judgments of various types of evidence of value. If the accountant has any area of expertise pertaining to value, it is in the field of evidence of value. The professional accountant uses his greatest skill, his most professional judgment, when he selects the types of evidence on which he will rely in ascertaining the amount of a specific asset or liability. The outline in Exhibit II gives explicit recognition to a variety of types of evidence of asset and liability amounts; we believe it includes the major categories that have a direct relation to the accountant's work. Note that the types of documents and communications media used to transmit the information to the accountant, such as invoices, price lists and newspapers, are ignored.

The amount of an asset may depend upon its physical quantity and the unit price attached to it. For example, measurements of commodity stocks and plant assets typically require measures of these two factors. The outline provides for evidence of both. Categories I and

## Exhibit II

TYPES OF EVIDENCE OF ASSET VALUE

I. Face or Nominal amount of a cash item

II. Contractual evidence

III. Market prices
  A. Exit prices
    1. Current
      a. Entity participated in establishing price
      b. Entity did not participate
    2. Past
      a. Entity participated in establishing price
      b. Entity did not participate
  B. Entry prices
    1. Current
      a. Entity participated in establishing price
      b. Entity did not participate
    2. Past
      a. Entity participated in establishing price
      b. Entity did not participate
  C. Price Indexes
    1. Specific (narrow) index (current entry prices)
    2. General (broad) measuring unit index

IV. Physical observation and count of quantities
  A. By entity personnel
  B. By external personnel as reported to entity

V. Miscellaneous statistical evidence
  A. Provided by entity personnel
  B. From external sources

II apply mostly to assets that have no separable quantity and price factors involved in their measurement. Category III includes prices only; categories IV and V relate primarily to unpriced quantities. Receiving reports and physical inventory sheets are examples of documents that transmit type IV-A evidence to accountants. Statements from brokers and independent warehousemen may reflect type IV-B evidence. Type V-A evidence provides much of the basis for estimates of bad debts and lives of amortizable assets. Type V-B evidence from appraisers or trade associations may also be used by accountants in connection with asset lives.

We contend that these types of evidence constitute the building blocks from which measurement methods are constructed. In accounting, a *measurement method* is a procedure for utilizing one or more types of evidence in ascertaining the amount of an asset or liability or the change in the amount of an asset or a liability. A *measurement* is both the act of measuring and the specific number resulting from the application of a measurement method to an object (asset or liability) in a particular case. A *measure* is the general result of applying a measurement method. The phrases used to identify measures (and variations thereof) listed in Exhibit III may also be used as short symbols for the related measurement methods. Thus, net realizable value is a common measure of asset amounts and is a measurement method that requires evidence of the physical quantity of goods on hand, the current entry prices for services required to sell those goods and the current exit price of the commodity. If an accountant finds evidence of 1,000 units of a commodity on hand, an exit market price of $8 and costs of selling of 50¢ per unit and makes the calculation $1,000($8 - .50) = $7,500$, his measurement method is net realizable value and $7,500 is his measurement of the stock of this commodity. Net realizable value is also the measure of asset amount the accountant has chosen to use. Exhibit III outlines some of the more likely measures of assets (and measurement methods).

The next step in our inquiry is to examine the relationships among the measurement methods we have recognized and between the resulting measures and our concept of value. Determining the amount of an asset by *counting the face value of cash items* is a highly relevant measurement method. These cash items are currently available to pay investors or to use in other ways that may appear more desirable and involve no material probability of loss. All noncash assets involve significant measurement problems. In the case of receivables, measurements of *future cash flows* involve a tradeoff between relevance and reliability. To achieve the highest degree of relevance in one figure, we must sacrifice at least a little reliability. We must either ignore the probability that the promised future cash flow will not materialize (and, thus, report claims to cash instead of the future cash flows decision-makers need to know) or estimate uncollectibles (and report

**Exhibit III**

MEASURES OF ASSETS AND TYPES OF EVIDENCE UTILIZED

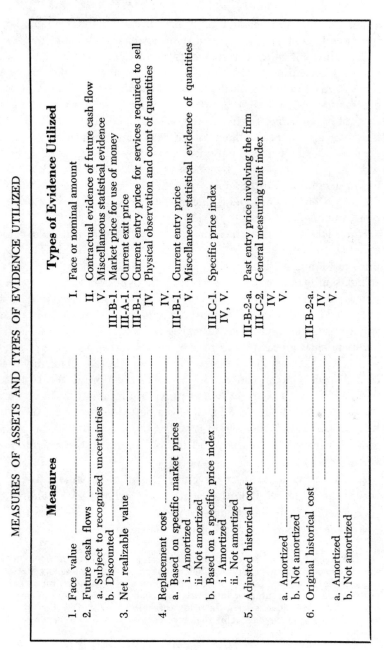

| Measures | | Types of Evidence Utilized |
|---|---|---|
| 1. Face value | I. | Face or nominal amount |
| 2. Future cash flows | | |
|   a. Subject to recognized uncertainties | II. | Contractual evidence of future cash flow |
| | V. | Miscellaneous statistical evidence |
|   b. Discounted | III-B-1. | Market price for use of money |
| 3. Net realizable value | III-A-1. | Current exit price |
| | III-B-1. | Current entry price for services required to sell |
| | IV. | Physical observation and count of quantities |
| 4. Replacement cost | IV. | |
|   a. Based on specific market prices | III-B-1. | Current entry price |
| | V. | Miscellaneous statistical evidence of quantities |
|     i. Amortized | | |
|     ii. Not amortized | | |
|   b. Based on a specific price index | III-C-1. | Specific price index |
| | IV, V. | |
|     i. Amortized | | |
|     ii. Not amortized | | |
| 5. Adjusted historical cost | III-B-2-a. | Past entry price involving the firm |
| | III-C-2. | General measuring unit index |
| | IV. | |
| | V. | |
|   a. Amortized | | |
|   b. Not amortized | | |
| 6. Original historical cost | III-B-2-a. | |
| | IV. | |
| | V. | |
|   a. Amortized | | |
|   b. Not amortized | | |

a net amount that cannot be relied upon as the true amount of future collections). Then, we must either select a discount rate (which is probably not quite correct) or we must fail to discount (thereby omitting the information available on the timing of the future cash flows). Accountants typically assume that they can improve upon the contractual amount of the future cash flow as a measure of asset amount by adjusting for uncertainty (uncollectibles). We believe that they can also improve their future cash flow measurements by discounting if the waiting period is material; a delay in a cash flow reduces its asset amount by a quantity that can be calculated with useful accuracy. Furthermore, the addition of undiscounted amounts due at different times yields a sum that has no definite meaning at a point in time.

Now, let us consider measurements at the *net realizable value* of an asset on a market in which it is expected to be sold. The current price in a highly developed and competitive market, less a current calculation of minor selling costs, can be expected to be a useful surrogate for the present value of the future cash flows that will be produced by this asset. The most likely defects in such a net realizable value arise from limitations in market quotations as single-valued and independent representations of the market price, probable changes in the market price prior to sale, a change in the sale plan, the absence of a discount factor and errors in the calculation of the costs to be deducted from the current selling price. By reference to these defects, we can see that net realizable value is a better surrogate for discounted future cash flows if the market is active and competitive,[7] the probable asset holding period is short and the remaining costs involved in converting the asset to cash are minor.

*Replacement cost* of an inventory item is an alternative to net realizable value. Full replacement cost, including all holding costs such as cost of capital, is equal to net realizable value (net of holding costs) in competitive equilibrium. This relationship is shown by

---

[7] The importance of the competitive feature is obvious when we note that a sloping demand curve yields marginal revenue less than the selling price. This suggests that a beginning inventory may contribute an incremental future cash flow less than the average future selling price, especially if the inventory is greater than is needed to avoid loss of sales. In many cases, this may weaken the relevance of net realizable value to the point that replacement cost would be the preferable measurement method.

Exhibit IV, which illustrates both the cost accumulation view of inventories in a manufacturing firm (starting at the lower left) and the receipt offset view (starting at upper right). If the two approaches fail to meet, a pure profit or loss is involved. The chart reflects the various stages in the operating cycle and relates to a product that meets the qualifications for measurement at net realizable value in its finished good stage. In traditional terminology, the accountant is said to "recognize revenue" when he elects to "jump the gap" between the two measurement approaches. Note that the gap is likely to be positive if some items of cost, such as cost of capital and general administrative costs, are completely omitted from the cost categories listed at the right-hand edge of the chart.[8] Under these circumstances, the gap would not represent pure profit.

The preceding discussion of the relationship between future cash flows, net realizable value and replacement cost pertains to stocks of commodities involved in the operating cycle of manufacturing or merchandising firms. In the case of necessary inventories of stock-in-trade, net realizable value appears to be more closely related to future cash flows than is replacement cost. Net realizable value is also closely related to future cash flows in the cases of securities and plant assets held for sale rather than use (e.g., a retired machine). In this latter case, replacement cost seems to be particularly irrelevant.

In another set of cases, replacement cost appears to be more directly related to the asset's effect upon future cash flows. If the absence of an asset would not affect future sales but would only require greater future acquisitions (by production or purchase), its differential cash flow effect appears to be equal to future acquisition cost. Present acquisition cost may be viewed as a good surrogate for future acquisition cost. Net realizable value presumably is not a good candidate in these cases if the presence or absence of the asset will not affect future sales. We believe this situation is typical of raw materials inventories and nonobsolete, fully utilized plant assets. The incremental effect on future cash flows from having one more or one fewer units on hand would be the cash effect of acquiring one fewer or one more unit in

---

[8] The usual reason for omitting the cost of any necessary input from product costs to be compared with product revenues is inability to associate the input with specific products with useful accuracy.

## Exhibit IV

### RELATIONSHIP BETWEEN NET REALIZABLE VALUE AND REPLACEMENT COST

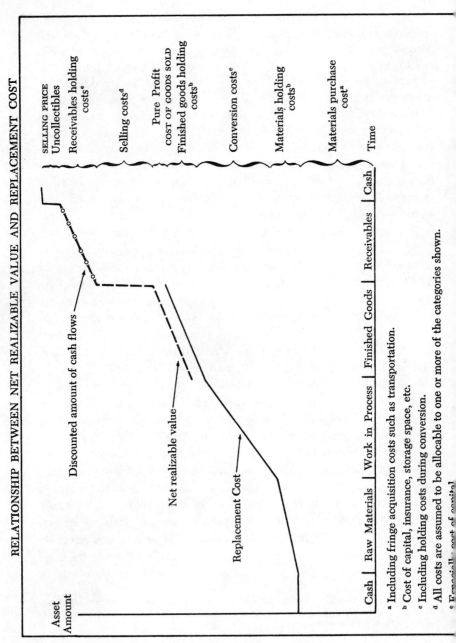

SELLING PRICE
Uncollectibles
Receivables holding costs[e]

Selling costs[d]

Pure Profit
COST OF GOODS SOLD
Finished goods holding costs[b]

Conversion costs[c]

Materials holding costs[b]

Materials purchase cost[a]

Time

Discounted amount of cash flows

Net realizable value

Replacement Cost

Asset Amount

Cash | Raw Materials | Work in Process | Finished Goods | Receivables | Cash

[a] Including fringe acquisition costs such as transportation.
[b] Cost of capital, insurance, storage space, etc.
[c] Including holding costs during conversion.
[d] All costs are assumed to be allocable to one or more of the categories shown.
[e] Especially cost of capital

the future. We have applied this sort of "disappearing asset" approach to a few other cases with the results appearing in Exhibit V.

The other two major measurement methods listed in Exhibit III—adjusted historical cost and historical cost—may be admitted to the accountant's tool kit because of their relationship to replacement cost. Adjusted historical cost differs from current replacement cost by the change in the real price of the asset, while historical cost (unadjusted) differs by the change in the money price. (Adjusted historical cost is historical cost adjusted by the percentage change in an index reflecting changes in the size of the monetary unit between acquisition date and the measurement date.) Since the money price of assets typically changes more than the real price, we consider adjusted historical cost to be more closely related to replacement cost than is historical cost. We should also recognize that the cost-based measurement methods may be justified as reflections of minimum value judgments by the management. Replacement cost is relevant on this basis if the management is purchasing similar assets relatively currently. Adjusted historical cost reflected a minimum value judgment at acquisition date. Exhibit VI summarizes the foregoing discussion of relationships between measurement methods.

We conclude that measurement methods can be ranked in order of relevance and that the array of Exhibit III is generally the proper rank order. The major exception involves nonmonetary assets held for "operating" purposes but whose absence would not result in a loss of operating revenues. A differential analysis indicates that replacement cost frequently is more relevant than net realizable value for such assets.

Several caveats should be recorded before we move on. The inclusion of net realizable value as a highly relevant measurement method for external reporting is dependent upon the interpretation that it must be based on a market in which the firm expects to sell the asset. Possible but improbable sources of net realizable values do not deserve such high ranking. (In fact, they would seem to have no place at all in a single-valued, external reporting system.) Furthermore, neither the order of the Exhibit III listing nor the right-hand column of Exhibit V is meant as a recommended application of any measurement method. Only relevance has been considered; the other major criterion—reliability—has not been considered in ranking the methods.

## Exhibit V

### REVIEW OF SOME POSSIBLE DIFFERENTIAL EFFECTS UPON A FIRM IF A SPECIFIED TYPE OF ASSET DISAPPEARED

| Asset Held | Possible Activity Effects of Disappearance | Possible Financial Effects | One Possible Surrogate Measurement Method |
|---|---|---|---|
| Receivables | Less payoff to investors<br>More external financing<br>Reduced scope of operations | Difference in future cash flow to or from investors | Discounting "expected value" of future cash flows |
| Marketable securities | Same as above | Same as above | Discounting future cash flows or net realizable value |
| "Real" assets needed to maintain operations | A. Reduce usage<br>  1. Internal use<br>    a. Substitute another input<br>    b. Reduce output and sales<br>  2. External use (sales)<br><br>B. Delay usage and increase future acquisitions<br>  1. Internal use<br>    a. Increase future production<br>    b. Increase future purchases<br>  2. External use (sales)<br>    a. Increase future production<br>    b. Increase future purchases | <br><br>Incur higher cost of substitute<br><br>Loss of future net realizable value<br>Loss of future net realizable value<br><br><br><br>Disruption costs and future production costs<br>Disruption costs and future acquisition costs<br><br>Goodwill loss and future production costs<br>Goodwill loss and future acquisition costs | <br><br>Present replacement cost of asset held<br>Present net realizable value<br>Present net realizable value<br><br><br><br>Present replacement cost by production<br>Present replacement cost by purchase<br><br>Present replacement cost by production<br>Present replacement cost by purchase |
| "Real" assets not needed to maintain operations | A. Reduce sale of "excess"<br><br>B. Increase future acquisitions | Loss of future net realizable value<br><br>Future replacement cost less holding costs saved | Present net realizable value<br><br>Present replacement cost |

## Exhibit VI

RELATIONSHIPS BETWEEN ASSET VALUE AND
ASSET MEASUREMENT METHODS

| Measurement Method | Relationship Justifying Its Use | Incremental Error versus Previous Method |
|---|---|---|
| Counting cash items. | Direct component of entity value. | |
| Future cash flows with allowances for failures and time. | Direct component of entity value marred only slightly by errors in estimating failures and in selecting proper discount rate. | Inaccurate estimate of uncollectibles, discount rate probably unsuitable. |
| Net realizable value in market in which asset is to be sold. | Current price in a highly developed market, less a current estimate of minor future costs, is a good surrogate for net future cash flows. | Inaccurate estimate of future costs, choice from range of market prices, firm's effect on market, change in price or costs prior to sale. |
| Replacement cost: | | |
| A. If absence of asset would reduce future sales. | Full replacement cost (including cost of capital) equals NRV (net of COC) in competitive equilibrium.* | Pure profit ($\pm$) due to imperfect competition or disequilibrium. |
| B. If absence of asset would increase future acquisitions. | Good surrogate for future cash outflows avoided by presence of asset and for cost of using asset (needed for cost minimization decisions).* | Not comparable. |
| Historical cost adjusted for change in measuring unit. | Surrogate for replacement cost, difference depending upon real price changes.* | Differs from replacement cost if real price has changed. |
| Historical cost stated in original number of monetary units. | Surrogate for replacement cost, difference depending upon real price changes and change in measuring unit, i.e., money price changes.* | Ignores fluctuations in the size of the measuring unit. |

* Cost-based methods may also be defended on the ground that management has judged the asset to be worth more than its cost.

We should also note that Exhibit V is not complete; it merely illustrates the nature of activity relevance of measurement methods.

One final observation about a relationship between measurement methods may be made here. In the case of receivables, net realizable value in the normal course of operations (rather than by quick sale or assignment) is, from a practical point of view, essentially the same as the discounted amount of future cash flows. If the net realizable value of receivables is net of carrying costs (mainly cost of capital) and uncollectibles, and if discounted future cash flows omit uncollectibles, the only conceptual difference would seem to be between cost of capital and discount—a difference which may disappear in practice.

This review of relationships among measurement methods and asset values reveals two practical views of relevant asset amounts, both based on the concept of present values of future cash flows. In an idealized decision-making environment, future cash inflows are assets, and future cash outflows are equities. If the decision-maker knows the times and amounts of the future cash inflows an asset will produce in each use under consideration, he has all the information he is likely to need about that asset. The times and amounts of future cash flows are the principals for some managerial decisions involving an asset, such as the sell-or-hold decision. The expression of the time and amount in one figure for each asset and the addition of such assets to one meaningful sum requires discounting. The discounted value of the future cash flows pertaining to an asset may be thought of as either an excellent surrogate for the times and amounts of those flows or a single-valued principal. Reliable discounted values are valuable data for use in the decisions of secondary beneficiaries of entity asset values, i.e., investors in the entity's securities. The accountant must seek reliable evidence of such discounted values. Such evidence may be found in contracts and in prices in markets in which assets are expected to be sold. Backward-looking measurements, such as replacement cost, adjusted historical cost and historical cost are poor surrogates for discounted values of future cash inflows. Where we have been is of interest only if it gives us our best clue as to where we are going; it is a pale substitute for reliable evidence of what is likely to happen.

The other view of relevant asset amounts picks up where the first leaves off. In the cases of many assets held for internal use, reliable evidence of their contributions to future cash inflows is unavailable. Furthermore, accountants encounter substantial practical difficulties in associating future selling, administrative and manufacturing overhead costs with specific assets in order to make the deductions necessary to obtain net realizable value. Net realizable values of many assets, such as supplies, minor raw materials and depreciable assets, via use in operations are not useful in current managerial processes because of formidable conceptual and practical difficulties; managers do not and cannot use them. Net realizable value of such assets via immediate sale, if immediate sale is improbable, is not likely to be a valuable output of the accounting system for use by managers and is not likely to represent a useful statement to the stockholder of what his share of stock represents. Another view of asset value appears to be more useful in such cases.

The contribution to a firm's future cash position that will be made by most assets held for internal use is by way of reducing future cash outflows, not by increasing future cash inflows. While it is possible for a stock of raw materials or a machine to make a distinct difference in the firm's future sales, many production operations have sufficient routing flexibility (alternative methods) and timing flexibility through "built-in holds" (inventories) to permit the firm to achieve the same future cash inflows regardless of the presence or absence of a specific input stock at a specific date. The differential effect of the presence or absence of the asset will show up in future acquisition costs, not in future revenues. The value of a stock of early-stage inputs comes from their contribution to the maintenance of operations with lower future cash outflows than would otherwise be required. The accountant should work towards reporting such a value, or a reliable surrogate, to investors rather than engage in the futile exercise of attempting to find direct evidence of future cash flows or the irrelevant exercise of reporting liquidation values of assets held for use.

But more importantly, recognition that assets held for use will affect the firm's future cash position by reducing future cash outflows leads us to the close surrogate—present replacement cost—which can make a great contribution to *costing* and to *cost minimization decisions*. A unit of a needed raw material, supply or machine that is on hand is a unit that need not be purchased in the future. When a manager wants to know the cost of using a unit of a regularly-used, scarce resource, he wants to know what difference it will make if he uses more or less of it. Since more or less use typically means more or less will be acquired in the future, future replacement cost is the relevant environmental variable; present replacement cost is a good surrogate. We believe that the most important use of measurements of the amounts of nonobsolete assets held for use is in cost minimization and other decisions requiring knowledge of the cost of using resources. We believe that replacement cost is by far the most reliable surrogate for the true cost of using such a resource. For this reason, we do not lament the unavailability of a reliable discounted value or a relevant and reliable net realizable value. If a penny saved is as good as a penny earned and if a cash outflow avoided is as good as a cash inflow, replacement cost of an asset held for use is as relevant as net realizable value of an asset held for sale in its existing form.

We conclude that the order in which the measurement methods are listed in Exhibit III is their order of relevance to the general run of managerial decisions and decisions of external investors but that the list begins with replacement cost when it is applied to that major class of nonmonetary resources held for "internal use" rather than for direct sale.

## IV. On Additivity and Subjectivity

The property we seek to measure is the differential effect of an asset or liability on the present value of the firm's future cash flows. Recognizing that direct measurements of this property are seldom feasible, we accept a variety of types of evidence of the target property. Some of the amounts thus selected are relatively accurate indicators of the target property; some are quite inaccurate. We intend, of course, to omit those that are not usefully accurate. We cannot expect the sum to have a smaller absolute error than that in the least accurate component, although offsetting errors may yield a smaller net error (but cumulative errors may yield a very large net error). We cannot hope for perfection in the measurement of the present value of a business enterprise any more than space scientists can hope for perfection in measuring the density of the moon's surface at a point chosen for a future landing, but in both cases, we can hope for a degree of accuracy that makes the measurements useful. While we may be able to make a more accurate measure of another property, such as the proceeds from a near future liquidation of the firm or the density of the moon's surface at the point of a past landing, we may well conclude that a rough measure of a relevant property is more useful than a precise measure of an irrelevant property.[9]

Several of the procedures that we have called measurement methods (e.g., net realizable value, historical cost) yield what might be called surrogate measures of an asset's discounted value. The use of surrogate measures in accounting almost assures imperfect representation of the principal. The addition of amounts derived from several different surrogate measures is an additional blemish, because it makes adjustment for systematic bias (in a surrogate as a representation of a principal) more difficult. But "... the fact that a representation is imperfect does not necessarily mean that it is totally useless. ... This is fortunate for those who design accounting information systems since if an imperfect representation were totally useless, it would be virtually impossible to develop any workable accounting information system."[10] Additivity can be overemphasized at the cost of reduced relevance or reliability. While it is true that adding the replacement cost of one asset to the net realizable value of another yields neither a total replacement cost nor a total net realizable value, this observation is of limited assistance to an accountant who has no reliable data on the replacement cost of certain assets and no reliable data on the net realizable value of others. Furthermore, for a myriad of specific managerial decisions, all useful data that it is feasible to accumulate in the accounts may be based on only one measurement method despite a mixed balance sheet; to pass up the most relevant data in such cases because of the additivity argument would indeed be foolish. Furthermore, those of us who believe that "consistency in objective is to be preferred to consistency in method"[11] can argue that imperfect measures of a common property—present value—arrived at by different

[9] Or as Sterling puts it, "A guess at a relevant figure is infinitely more valuable than a precise and objective irrelevancy." Robert R. Sterling, "Conservatism: The Fundamental Principle of Valuation in Traditional Accounting," *Abacus* (December 1967), p. 131.

[10] Yuji Ijiri, *The Foundations of Accounting Measurement* (New York: Prentice-Hall, 1967), p. 13 .

[11] Raymond J. Chambers, *Accounting, Evaluation and Economic Behavior* (New York: Prentice-Hall, 1966), p. 260.

methods meet the technical requirements for additivity. Various degrees of imperfection in the individual measurements do not render their sum completely meaningless or useless.

Perhaps an analogy will help. Suppose a person is planning a motor trip from San Francisco to Colon, Panama and wants to know the distance to help him judge the driving time and the gasoline consumption. Suppose that on the Sunday that he is making these judgments, the information available to him is limited and varied but he is able to accumulate the following data:

(1) The distance from San Francisco to the Mexican border at Tijuana, according to an oil company map he had in his car is                                     530 miles

(2) A friend who recently had driven from Tijuana to Mexicali said that he recorded the distance as 125 miles on his odometer.                           125 miles

(3) A Mexican-American friend who once was traffic manager for a Mexican bus company had an old fare schedule showing a fare of 600 pesos for the trip from Mexicali to Mexico City. He said that the company set its fares on the basis of 25 centavos per kilometer and then rounded it off to the nearest peso. On this basis he thought the distance from Mexicali to Mexico City was 2,400 kilometers. At roughly .62 miles per kilometer this came to       1,488 miles

(4) The Mexican-American friend also had an old map of southern Mexico. The distance figures from town to town were very difficult to read, but from what could be read plus a few guesses at last digits it appeared to be 968 kilometers from Mexico City to the Guatemala border.[12] Multiplied by .62 this came to approximately                        600 miles

(5) A banana company executive said that when he was stationed in Costa Rica and had his own plane he once flew from San Jose, Costa Rica to Guatemala City in 4 hours. He was confident that he had

---

[12] The friend said a new road saves "a few kilometers" on one stretch.

maintained a constant air speed of 200 miles per hour and thought there was only a slight breeze off his left wing-tip. 800 miles

(6) An atlas with a scale of miles showing 100 miles per inch revealed that it was one inch from the Mexico-Guatemala border to Guatemala City and ¾ inch from San Jose to the Panama border. 175 miles

(7) A call to the Panamanian Consul General's home brought forth the belief that the distance from the Costa Rica-Panama border to Colon was between 200 and 250 miles. The atlas map showed 1.9 inches. 225 miles

Total 3,943 miles

(8) A globe showed the distance from San Francisco to Los Angeles to be 400 nautical miles and the distance from Los Angeles to Colon as 2,600 miles, for a total by sea of 3,000 nautical miles. At 1.13 land miles per nautical mile this amounts to 3,390 miles.

The 3,943 miles is a measure of the road mileage from San Francisco to Colon that is unlikely to be correct to the nearest mile, but it may be more useful for making decisions about driving from one city to the other than the measure of sea mileage, despite the latter's neatness. We believe that balance sheet and income statement sums and differences based on the evidential approach are likely to be more useful to decision-makers than would similar figures consistently based on a historical cost, adjusted historical cost, replacement cost or net realizable value method of measurement.

Some readers may feel that measuring an asset or a liability by reference to the expected future cash flow related to the item places too much reliance on future events. But in what sense does it rely on the future? It relies upon the same type of evidence as does net realizable value, viz., a past transaction price, so surely, it cannot be said to be any less objective than net realizable value. The fact of the matter is that the *usefulness* of all accounting measurements is dependent upon future events. If the debtor fails to pay, if the cash box is stolen, or if the inventory is burned, the asset amount based on contractual evidence of future cash flows, counting cash, or current market value will turn out to be a poor basis for an investor's predictions. Net realizable value of an inventory is not useful information unless it can be relied upon as an indication of what will or could happen. It is useful as a surrogate for future cash flows that will or could happen; it is not useful because the manager or investor must know net realizable value. Similarly, when product costing is done on the basis of replacement cost, the information is only useful if it is a good surrogate for the future cash disbursement that is caused by using the resource in question today. Even historical cost is a surrogate for future cash flows; we certainly do not need to know historical cost per se. The usefulness of all of these measurements is dependent upon future events; their basis is factual information from the past.

If the value of accounting measurements is dependent upon future events, by how much do we reduce their value by explicitly making use of reliable evidence of what will happen rather than regarding such evidence as tainted and unfit for user consumption? We certainly would look foolish refusing to utilize evidence of what will happen in connection with receivables and payables, telling thousands of stockholders around the world that only they are in a position to make such predictions, that we accountants can only report the December 31 net realizable value (via factoring?) or historical cost (including allocated selling and administrative costs?) of receivables and historical receipt of, say, wages payable. There is nothing about measurement, accounting, economics, finance or management that rules out reliance on evidence of future events in making accounting measurements.

Nor can accountants reasonably omit judgments made by parties within the firm, e.g., estimates of uncollectible receivables or of depreciable lives. Our much-admired market values reflect judgments of sacrifices, alternatives and utility. There is no fundamental difference between judgments made by accountants and judgments made by buyers and sellers, at least none that says one is objective and the other subjective. Either may be biased. The only objective aspect of a market price is that a transaction did occur at that price. The price itself, which is the measure in which we are interested, is not even an explicit opinion of the worth of the good; the buyer thinks it is worth more than the price; the seller, less. The relationship between the judge(s) and the entity does not, by itself, determine which judgments are useful and which useless. The accounting process of selecting useful valuations must be based on assessments of relevance and reliability after considering a number of environmental conditions, including, but not limited to, the relation of the evaluator to the entity. How much risk of bias and how much subjectivity can be accepted is partly dependent upon the alternatives that are available. If the alternative is replacement or retirement accounting, internal estimates of asset lives may (or may not) be useful; their acceptability must be decided in the light of the attendant circumstances. Whether or not estimating asset lives is an accounting function is of little concern to us. We urge those who have a narrow view of the accounting function to be less concerned about overstepping the boundaries of that function and more concerned with providing useful information. "Any attempt to cope with the difficulties of measuring a property known to be relevant is preferable to any attempt to measure an entirely different property instead, unless the measure of a different property is the closest possible approximation to the measure of the desired property."[13]

The practical import of our argument may be elucidated by considering the following problem. You have been asked to prepare a balance sheet for the Company for use in determining the sale price of an ownership interest. Owner A has agreed to sell his 40% interest to Owner B, who already has a 15% interest, at its "book value based on sensible, but not necessarily generally accepted, principles of accounting." Mr. A and Mr. B are two of your best friends. You have been able to gather the data shown in Exhibit VII.

We believe that you would minimize the risk of losing a friend if you make use of several different measurement methods. We specifically recommend that you use the present value of future cash flows (discounted at 8%) for the notes receivable, undiscounted future cash flows for the cotton (based on the contract to sell), net realizable value for the cottonseed, replacement cost for the dress shop inventory

---

[13] Chambers, p. 231.

## Exhibit VII

**Company**
**Balance Sheet**
**December 31, 1969**

| | | | |
|---|---|---|---|
| Cash | $40,000 | Current Liabilities | $100,000 |
| Notes Receivable (See Note 1) | | Long-term Debt | 200,000 |
| Cotton (See Note 2) | | Total Liabilities | 300,000 |
| Cottonseed (See Note 3) | | | |
| Dress Shop Inventory (See Note 4) | | Owners' Equity | |
| Land (See Note 5) | | | |
| Total Assets | $_____ | Total Equities | $_____ |

NOTE 1. During the year the company sold a portion of its land for a cash amount and a mortgage note calling for payment of $20,000 per year each January 1 for 15 years. The state agriculture department's record of average interest rates on farm mortgages stands at 8%. The land had cost $22,000 when purchased in 1939. (See Note 5).

NOTE 2. The company operates a cotton farm and a gin for separating cotton fiber from the seeds. The company has contracted to sell the entire 1969 crop, consisting of 1,000,000 pounds, at a price of $.30 per pound for delivery to the buyer's loading and trucking crew at the company's gin between January 1 and January 15, 1970. This grade of cotton is quoted at $.28 per pound at the nearest wholesale market and the company would have to pay a trucker $2 per ton to haul it to market. The cost of growing and ginning the year's crop was $240,000.

NOTE 3. The cottonseed inventory of 600 tons consists of the entire year's crop (see Note 2). The local seed processing mill is currently paying $60 per ton and will pick it up at the seller's gin.

NOTE 4. The company operates a dress shop, Alice's Store, which caters to the local high school and college girls. The inventory has current marked prices amounting to $25,000. The historical cost of the inventory on a specific identification basis was $14,000; due to several markdowns by suppliers, the replacement cost of the goods is $13,000. Operating expenses have varied between 39 and 45% of sales in recent months.

NOTE 5. The company's land was acquired for $50,000 in 1939 when the county index of crop land prices was one-third of its present level.

and replacement cost computed with the aid of the land price index for the land. In the absence of the specific price index, we would have chosen adjusted historical cost in preference to historical cost.

## V. Conclusion

Measurement of net asset items is still the fundamental problem underlying most of the controversies in accounting. The profession's refusal to face up to this problem has unnecessarily prolonged the disastrous diversity of inventory practices in similar circumstances; it has driven security analysts to cash flow; it has split the business community over the purchase-pooling issue.

We believe that a careful analysis of the needs of users of accounting data will disclose that the property of noncash assets that is most relevant to most decisions of investors and managers is their incremental effect upon the present value of the firm's future cash flows. Other measurement methods can be ranked behind discounting on the criterion of relevance. With these rankings in mind, the accountant can compare his assessment of the reliability with which several measures can be applied in the specific case against their relevance rankings and choose that measure which he believes will provide the most useful information.

# Response to
# The Relevance of Evidence of Cash Flows

*by* Oscar S. Gellein

HASKINS & SELLS

IT IS a pleasure to be here, and really a privilege to participate in the symposium. I am sure I will take much more away from it than I will bring to it. It is a special pleasure to discuss matters that may prevent new accounting fires rather than to be putting out the daily fires. I suppose many of you might expect a practitioner to extol the virtues of verifiability, conservatism, and realization—I am not going to do that. In the first place, I think these matters are of a much lower order than those things we are here to talk about. Their consideration must come later, however important they may be. So, I am laying them aside completely. Another thing is that, and here I agree with George Catlett, something needs to be done somewhere. There are just too many applications of historical cost in its ultimate sense that give what I deem to be some bad answers. I will not recite them. George Catlett mentioned several of them. I would speculate on one other aspect that he did not mention. It is my belief that rigid adherence to an historical cost basis of accounting was one of the things that permitted some of the alternatives to come into use. I cannot prove that, but I think it is true. By ignoring the market situation in which business was operating and the change in values in the market, historical cost, or rigid application of it, just could not stand up in its complete form and so we saw some alternatives come into practice.

Let me first say something about relevance. I sometimes wonder if relevance in the first instance is not limited to simply that which is

70

necessary to identify or define the accounting population. Then the question is, it seems to me, whether relevance can be made operative in selecting and compiling data for financial statements from the population deemed relevant. In other words, does relevance help one with selection or does it simply assist in identifying the population from which a selection is made. I have a very difficult time in separating relevance from use. It seems to me that we have got to rank the uses that might be made of financial information, and having ranked those uses, then we have got to decide which ones of those uses we will attempt to meet, and how, and which ones we will not—and this I would think constitutes relevance as an operative factor. It may be, too, that we will have to build some irrationality (you might say, irrelevance) into our system of accounting. It may be that we cannot convince people to be rational, no matter how we try. I sometimes wonder if the accounting profession did not recognize that, in part, when it issued its Opinion on earnings per share. I do not mean the Opinion is irrational. I am simply wondering if maybe some irrational uses of P/E ratios and multiples were not accepted and therefore were built into the conclusions.

Let me also say at the outset that I do not know what we ought to do about the structure of accounting. It may be that we will need a blend of the four accounting structures being discussed at this symposium. If it were a blend, we might not know conceptually what income is and the numbers comprising it might not be additive, but perhaps it would be operational. I would urge a structure for making income understandable to those interested. It is hard to see how something that is not understood by a user can be relevant to that user's interests.

Well now, let me turn to George Staubus' paper. I thought that this was a very thoughtfully prepared paper, almost ingeniously organized, especially in terms of what George purported to do, that is, to look at the relevance of the evidence of present value of future cash flow. My comments—I guess they are more questions than they are anything else—start with his basic hypothesis, (p. 48) where it is stated, in effect, that the most relevant property of an asset or liability is the incremental effect which its existence might have upon the present value of the future cash flows of the company. I have a question about this incremental aspect. Does this mean that if every asset and liability is included in the balance sheet on this basis, the net assets will show the present value of the future cash flows of the company itself? It seems to me it would not. For example, suppose the company has only two assets, Asset A and Asset B, and both of them are necessary to have any future cash flow in the conduct of the business. Then, what is the incremental effect of Asset A and what is the incremental effect of Asset B? Offhand, it would seem that the sum of their separate incremental effects would be zero, but that their incremental effect as a combination of assets would be, presumably, something more than zero.

A second point that I wonder about is how the element of probability enters into the determination of income on the basis of present value of future cash flows. Does it come into the determination through the discounting rate? I would think not. I would think that would be trying to make the discount rate serve too many purposes, or at least mixed purposes, which seem not necessarily to relate. Again suppose that as to any given asset (I am not talking about measurement; I assume we can solve the measurement problem), it might be said with sixty percent probability that gross future cash inflow would be x dollars, but with forty percent probability, it would be y dollars, and suppose there is nothing in between. Maybe that is the fallacy, maybe there has to be something in between, I do not know. But if we assume that, then how do we arrive at the present value determination? Do we work from the one that has sixty percent probability that it will be x dollars or from the one that has forty percent probability that it will be y dollars? As to the rate itself, it would almost seem to me that in this system, the considerations relating to the rate of discount would be an important element in the over-all system. And I do not mean to be concerned at the moment with specific rates. Would we use, however, long term rates applicable to the company? Would we use short term rates when the term is short or do we use the same rate, without regard to the term of the series being discounted? Or, still further, in finding the present value of future cash flows, would we also use a future discount rate?

I have no quarrel with George's conclusions concerning the additive nature of surrogates. I see nothing to fight about in ascertaining stand-in measurements and then adding them, except that if the stand-ins are numerous and large, their total might better be described as a measurement from some system other than the one from which the surrogates were chosen.

And finally, I think the thing that perhaps I understand the least—and I will put it that way—is related to the income statement itself. What is income here? As a group of us were saying last night, it would help all of us to see four income statements in parallel columns, one under each system. I think I know what it would look like under historical cost, and Professor Bell gave an example of a current cost income statement. I have, I guess, the most trouble trying to see what it would look like in connection with future cash flows. I suppose there would be a revenue line and a cost of revenue line and a gross margin line, but there is one other element of it that sort of perplexes me. It almost seems to me that in this system there would be, shall I call it, front-end loading of income or instant income, which is a popular term these days. And my reasoning is this. At any given time with respect to any particular product, I would think as to the various buyers, that each would have a different measure of the present value of future cash flow with respect to that product. So some buyers would be buying at a price which is considerably below the present value of his future cash flow with respect to that asset. Let us say that a buyer has just bought it, and now we prepare the balance sheet immediately after purchase. Now it seems that income would be shown instantly. And if so, you see, there has been income without effort and without any change in the environment or the circumstances surrounding the company. Further, there would be the question of identifying the point in time when an asset would be recognized. In this system, it would seem that present value of future cash flows might get measured and recognized when a commitment had been made, perhaps even earlier.

# 4

# Evidence for a Market–Selling Price– Accounting System

*by* RAYMOND J. CHAMBERS
UNIVERSITY OF KANSAS
*on leave from* UNIVERSITY OF SYDNEY

## I. Schema

A SYSTEM is a contraption for doing one or more things. A well-designed system is a contraption for doing that or those things well. We cannot pretend we are designing a system, or repairing a system or modifying a system unless we have clearly in mind the things we intend it to do, and unless we are concerned with fashioning its parts or elements so that it does just those things. The design of the system is, thus, primarily dependent on what it is expected to produce.

A complex system is a contraption for doing complex things. Commonly, it consists of subsystems, each doing or designed to do its own thing, but each designed to fit into and be part of the complex system. No subsystem in a well-designed system is inconsistent with the whole system, and no subsystem is designed to do just the same thing as any other subsystem. If they were, we would not call such a system well-designed, for inconsistencies will require additional subsystems to offset them, and superfluous subsystems are just in the way, uneconomical.

For analytical purposes we may take for examination a system as large or as small as we please. But, if it is locked in with other systems or is part of a larger system, we will know little of it and, hence, have little chance of designing it well, unless we take account of the larger system of which it is a part.

The economic organization of a community is a system. We shall consider just some parts of it. To avoid cumbersome expression, we shall speak of two systems which are really subsystems of the whole economic organization: the F-system, a single firm; and the W-system, the rest of the world or community. And we shall speak only of the financial features of these two systems.

There is a subsystem of F which engages in trading relations (having financial characteristics) with W. Call it the transactions subsystem F(T). There is a subsystem of F which sets the framework of these transactions. Call it the managerial subsystem F(M). If transactions are many and the relations between F and W persist over time, there is a subsystem of F which keeps track of the transactions and relations between F and W. Call it the accounting subsystem F(A). If F is a well-designed system, each of its subsystems will engage smoothly with one another, without gaps, inconsistencies or irrelevancies, as the parts of any well-designed machine. F(T) concerns itself with market prices, buying and selling prices. F(M) sets the framework or policy within which F(T) operates. F(A) provides the information on what has occurred and the consequences of what has occurred in F(T), so that F(M) may vary the framework of F(T) from time to time. As F(T) engages with the system W in terms of buying and selling prices, the function of F(A) in the system F will be to accumulate, arrange and digest buying and selling price information. If F(A) produces any information which is not in the nature of a price, F(M) will have to convert it to price information or seek price information from other sources or guess what framework it should set for F(T) from time to time. The system F will not be a well-designed system.

The system W has subsystems which correspond with the subsystems of F, namely W(T), W(M) and W(A). As the two systems W and F engage through their transactions subsystems, both F(T) and W(T) will engage on the same terms; namely prices—and at any given time, the prices at that time. And F(A) and W(A) will produce information in terms of those prices if F(M) and W(M) are to set the subsequent framework or policy for F(T) and W(T).

Now in the system which is (W + F), no single F is indispensable.

W is larger than F; there may be other firms in W which can produce what F produces, consume what F consumes, employ the labor which F employs, use the money funds which F uses. F(M) must, therefore, set the framework for F(T) from time to time in the light of what is occurring in W and the expectations of the components of W(T) with which it presently engages and may find it useful to engage. And, because the system F is at any time in a specific financial state or relation to W, that state or relation is one of the premises on which F(M) must proceed in setting the framework for F(T); for, certainly W(M) will proceed on that basis.

Now, there are effects on F due to W which do not arise merely from transactions. When the prices of particular inputs to F change through events in the system (W + F), F(M) may vary the framework of F(T) in one or more ways—direct it to seek less expensive inputs, to raise output prices, to change the composition of what it buys and sells (i.e., the production mix)—according to the expectations of W entertained by F(M). Those changes in prices have immediate effects, notwithstanding that F may not replenish its "inventory" at any given price. Furthermore, when prices of all things rise or fall, the unit in which transactions (and hence, relations) are expressed acquires a different meaning than it had before with reference to goods and services.

If F(M) is to set the framework of F(T) on the basis, *inter alia*, of the present state of F, the present state of F must be defined so that it has reference to the ability of F(T) to procure the effects proposed by F(M). F(T) can procure those effects only by having cash or getting cash from W by the sale of what F has at the time. So that we can say that the present state of F is defined by reference to the selling prices of what it has at any time.

We will call F(A) a well-designed subsystem if it meets the requirements of the last two paragraphs.

We have said that one of the premises of F(M) in proceeding to choose a course to be followed by F(T) is the state of F at the time. There are many such possible courses—"sell this and buy that," "borrow this and buy that," "discharge this debt and incur that one." The state of F is a common premise for all. Which of these courses is deemed to be feasible depends on the expectations of F(M) regarding W; for

F(T) can only operate by engagements with W. Which of the feasible courses is deemed to be preferable to other feasible courses depends on what state of F at some future time is preferred by F(M) to other possible states at that time. Notice that these last two elements in the process of choice are non-factual; one relates to expectations of F(M) at a point of time, the other to a preference of F(M) based on expectations at a point of time.

Two features of the products of F(A) are distinctively different from these features of F(M). The recorded history of F, as developed by F(A) is, in a sense, continuous. Given one state, say at $t_0$, and the transactions and events between $t_0$ and $t_1$, the state at $t_1$ can be deduced. Thus, F(M) can discover states at any time by reference to F(A). If, although F(A) is a well designed system, it does not operate perfectly, its output can be readily checked externally from time to time by reference to the prices ruling in W. There is no such continuity or possibility of independent corroboration (and correction, if necessary) of the expectations and calculations which are contributory to choice. For, if F(M) expects F to be in a certain state at $t_1$ in the light of the actual state at $t_0$ and some expected events, there is no apparent way (in a varying world) of deducing either the actual state of F at $t_1$ or the expectation F(M) will entertain at $t_1$ or the state F will be in at $t_2$. The contingent nature of future events, and the reasonable requirement that F(M) will always proceed to calculate from the actual state at a point of time, entail that all calculations about the future will be temporally isolated events, making use of the knowledge of the present state and of such other market prices as are relevant. These calculations are necessary events, certainly, but unique and evanescent. It should scarcely be necessary to argue that there is no way of verifying the content of any statement or calculation about the future at the time the statement is made.

There is a further point, generally disregarded. All problems of project evaluation emphasize in some way the expected cash flows and the net present values. It is not universally correct to say that that project which has the greater net present value is to be preferred. It would always be the case if the horizon of calculation were the terminus of the whole venture and if no other condition required by W were violated up to that time. But, if F is to be a continuing system, then its state at any time must be such that W will continue to engage with it. Solvency, contractual or conventional leverage conditions and the capacity to make dividend payments are all part of the requirements of W, so that any preferred state must meet these requirements. There is, thus, a link between F(A) and W(T), which a well designed F(A) will serve.

The preceding style of analysis, of a line of argument given elsewhere in different terms, has been designed to bring under notice one major point. The products of any F(A) enter as premises into the processes of analysis and calculation of *other* parts of the systems F and W, many other parts. They will be related to many other prices. There is no way in which, if they are not cash amounts or prices themselves, they can be related to other prices. There is no way in which, if they are not contemporary prices themselves, they, or any combination of them, can be related to other prices which are contemporary. If any of them has any relation to the payment of any existing debt or the securing of any new debt, they must be in the nature of cash or have a cash equivalent.

The use of the impersonal idea of systems is intended to lift the argument away from the vague term "usefulness" which, though it is seldom defined, is running riot in the literature. I think it might be preferable to speak of functional information rather than of useful information. If we ask what is useful, we tend to suggest useful to someone; we are then confronted with the possibility that any piece of "information" may be said by someone to be useful. There is no way of tying practices down to a tight description of "useful." I am not sure the term "functional" is vastly superior. But, in the context of the description of the firm and its relations which I have just given, what it signifies is not hard to see. A piece of information is functional if it is a necessary premise of any other party in the systems F or W for any kind of calculation which that party wishes to make. And information relating to a financial state is functional if it can be confidently taken by any party as a basis for calculating backward, presently, or forward. Of course, if all F(A) subsystems are well-designed, their products can be used generally and with confidence throughout a community, for they will be uniform in substance and significance and equally relatable to one another and to all conceivable transactions at a given time.

## II. Inconsistencies Between Accounting Practice
## and Commercial Behavior

I came to my own conclusions on the inconsistencies between accounting practice and commercial behavior by a devious route. The kind of accounting commonly done is not consistent with the kind of data one ordinarily employs in one's own calculations. Nor with the kinds of analysis one finds in elementary economics. Yet, it is claimed, almost universally and by large groups of professional and academic people, that it yields useful information. One may satisfy oneself on the one hand by analysis or model-building. One may construct a theoretical system, necessarily on the basis of one's own presuppositions (original or learned; mostly learned). But, as accounting is a real-world phenomenon, there should be evidence, beyond oneself and one's convictions, of the inconsistency between accounting practice and commercial behavior, if indeed there is inconsistency.

The kind of evidence which would be acceptable, I decided, would be occurrences which arose more or less spontaneously. It would be better to avoid manufacturing evidence. Most forms of opinion inquiry, questionnaire or contrived experiment could be challenged on the ground that the way they were structured would "create" a situation biased in some way, or would "force" into play whatever sympathies and antipathies may surround customary or habitual practices. It would be better just to look, to see what was happening *independently of prompting in the particular direction of my own ideas*. There are many kinds of such evidence: What companies do in their accounting; what their chairmen or presidents say by way of augmenting or qualifying what their financial statements say; what businessmen say about accounting; what legal documents designed to protect the rights of contracting parties contain; what accountants and professional bodies say (since none of what they have said has been consciously directed towards or against my own ideas); what analysts do; what the information services provide; what economists say about accounting and the context in which accounting information is used; and so on.

It should be obvious that if one is looking at what goes on, the sayers and doers are acting free of the suspicion that what they say or do will be used in the particular way I choose to use it. On my part, therefore, the evidence is independent of me. Such a form of observation is similar, in this respect, to any form of strictly scientific inquiry.

It should also be obvious that some of the evidence will be indicative only. For example, if the practice in accounting is to use for one kind of asset a contemporary price, and for all other kinds of asset some other number or price, the use of a contemporary price in one instance is some evidence. But if, from many directions, there are such fragments of evidence, and if there are no such fragments of evidence in equal quantities for any alternative practice, we may consider the *convergence* of such evidence to be in the nature of empirical confirmation.

The remainder of this paper will present some of the indications. As there are so many possible sources of evidence, I cannot pretend to have examined all or any of them exhaustively. But I hold that the scraps I shall offer are mere samples or specimens of kinds of observation which could be made in great abundance by anyone who cares to look in similar directions. These scraps have come under my notice at different times over the past twenty years.[1] They have affected the views I have held from time to time, yielding at last what confidence I have in my present conclusions. They are drawn indiscriminately from the literature and practices of people in different countries who have been concerned with business and accounting in the kind of developed industrial economy with which we are familiar. As the conduct of *business* is substantially the same in such economies, the kind of accounting appropriate to that kind of business is the same kind. Drawing on illustrations from different economies enables one, therefore, to skirt the purely local habits and practices which have arisen from the idiosyncratic experiences of particular communities.

### III.  *Functional Information—Comprehensible Signals*

As we said in the introduction, when two or more parties are engaged in an operation in any sense interdependently, the communications between them are unlikely to produce responses appropriate to their positions unless those communications are understandable alike to all. Business managers, investors, financiers, analysts and advisers,

---

[1] Some of them have been used in earlier publications. The collection of some of these in *Accounting, Finance and Management* ( Sydney, Australia: Butterworth & Co., 1969) makes it easier to cite one source. I shall refer to these articles by the abbreviated reference *A.F.M.*

suppliers and customers and others are engaged in interdependent operations, giving and receiving money and other financial instruments of or relating to a given firm. All communications embodying amounts of money are understood in the normal course of affairs as having reference to the capacity to pay a price (e.g., a statement about cash holdings) or a reference to some price or prices expressed in money. As the structure of prices and the general level of prices change from time to time, any communication expressed in money is commonly interpretable only in the light of prices ruling at or about the time of the communication. And any money sum which is an aggregate of other sums will be interpretable only if the component sums and the aggregate are themselves prices or are relatable to prices at or about the same time. Among these communications are the financial statements which accountants prepare.

We might, therefore, expect to find some evidence of the use of contemporary prices or of amounts which can be directly related to contemporary prices. And we might expect to find signs of dissatisfaction with the use of other kinds of numbers, vacillation in the prescription and use of other kinds of numbers, and suggestions that the other kinds be supplemented or replaced by more or less contemporary numbers, if not contemporary prices.

## The Evidence

1. We do, in fact, find in the practice of accounting some contemporary monetary magnitudes. Universally, we find the actual present amounts of cash: and generally, we find the present amounts of receivables and payables, even though in some cases we may doubt the ways in which the amounts of receivables are determined. And we do find the use of market prices in respect to inventories at least some of the time. The lower of cost or market, and the use of net realizable value, and the outright use of market prices in some trades, all signify that market prices are indeed used at least some of the time.

2. We do, in fact, find vacillation in the general prescriptions relating to the valuation of assets on other bases. In the recommendations and prescriptions of professional bodies, we find numerous alternative valuation bases mentioned. No firm grounds for any of the

alternatives are given. Many alternatives are not even in the nature of contemporary prices. And the choice is left open to accountants or managers, without any guidance in the prescriptions. Analysis of the accounts of almost every company will show that the same components have been valued on different bases through time. Reference to the consecutive issues of *Accounting Trends and Techniques* will show the extent of this vacillation. *Trends* of 1967 shows that in 1960, 1965, 1966 there were 54, 43, 29 cases, respectively, of "changes in consistent application of generally accepted principles of accounting."[2] It can confidently be said, from the tabulations throughout *Trends*, that changes in particulars are much more numerous. Recent shifts in depreciation accounting and merger accounting are conspicuous examples of idiosyncratic accounting. All such changes are unaccountable, except on the hypothesis that there is no confident belief in the functional quality of any one of the methods used, the newly adopted or the method rejected—for while some companies are adopting one method, others are rejecting it.

3. Bearing on the same point, we do find strong suggestions that steps should be taken to reduce "unnecessary diversity" in accounting methods. The suggestions have come from leaders of the accounting profession and from officials of the SEC. The argument for "narrowing the differences" is sometimes couched in terms of improving the comparability of the resulting figures, which is just one facet of interpreting the figures or producing comprehensible figures.

4. We do, in fact, find critical comments on the use in accounting of figures other than contemporary prices in the reports of presidents and chairmen of companies. References to a number of examples from the United Kingdom, the United States and Australia are given in "The Formal Basis of Business Decisions"[3] and in *The Function and Design of Company Annual Reports.*[4]

---

[2] *Accounting Trends & Techniques*, Twenty-First Edition (New York: American Institute of Certified Public Accountants, 1967), Table 4, p. 273.

[3] Chambers, *A.F.M.*, p. 70.

[4] R. J. Chambers, *The Function and Design of Company Annual Reports* (Sydney, Australia: The Law Book Co., 1955).

5. Every argument for replacement price accounting and price level adjusted accounting is, at bottom, an argument for approximating figures which are currently interpretable. (We are not concerned at this point with other elements of these proposals.) There have been and are many supporters of both among professional accountants and academics. The Institute of Chartered Accountants in England and Wales in 1952 produced Recommendation XV "Accounting in Relation to Changes in the Purchasing Power of Money." The Institute of Cost and Works Accounts (England) produced in 1952 *The Accountancy of Changing Price Levels*. The Association of Certified and Corporate Accountants produced in 1952 *Accounting for Inflation*. The American Accounting Association supported the works on the effects of price level changes of Mason and Jones in the mid-fifties.[5] In 1963 we had ARS 6,[6] which incidentally reports a number of companies, in different countries, whose accounting is in the direction we are discussing. More recently we have the APB Statement No. 3.[7] The number of individual supporters of one or the other of these proposals and the number of articles supporting them have never been estimated. Both must be large. There have been eminent individual contributors, from commerce, the profession and the universities in Germany, the Netherlands, Japan, Britain, the United States and Australia, and no doubt in many other countries, too.

6. The common statutory requirement that certain kinds of companies shall publish periodically a statement of financial position and results which shall contain no untrue statements or omissions likely to mislead (or other equivalent words) is a pointless requirement, unless the statements so published are commonly interpretable. The broad foundation of such a law is, that if men pursue their

---

[5] Perry Mason, *Price Level Changes and Financial Statements: Basic Concepts and Methods* (Columbus, Ohio: American Accounting Association, 1956). Ralph Coughenour Jones, *Price Level Changes and Financial Statements: Case Studies of Four Companies* (Evanston, Illinois: American Accounting Association, 1955).

[6] Staff of the Accounting Research Division, American Institute of Certified Public Accountants, *Reporting the Financial Effects of Price-Level Changes*, Accounting Research Study No. 6 (New York: American Institute of Certified Public Accountants, Inc., 1963).

[7] Accounting Principles Board, *APB Statement No. 3*, "Financial Statements Restated for General Price-Level Changes" (New York: American Institute of Certified Public Accountants, Inc., 1969).

own interests knowledgeably, the welfare of a community as a whole is advanced. The narrower foundation is, that if each investor or lender is periodically informed of the affairs of companies in which he invests or may invest, he can protect his interest. As the quantities *and* the prices of company assets rise and fall, no investor can be informed by statements which embody the effects of changes in quantities but not of changes in prices. To so report would be to make an "omission likely to mislead." The law clearly seems to contemplate financial statements which are presently interpretable and presently indicative, because they are in terms of present prices. Writing close to the date of the Securities Act of 1933, Professor Sanders was of the opinion that Congress "doubtless was thinking of the balance sheet mainly as . . . a statement of *present* conditions."[8] As creditors are quitted by cash payments, and as investors may divest themselves of their interests by sale of their "share" or by liquidation of a company or by swapping securities, protection is, in fact, assured only by using present resale market prices of assets in statements of present condition.

7. Such general publicity laws have been very loosely interpreted, or misinterpreted, in practice. Following notable instances of the divergence of published "information" from factual information and consequential losses by investors, more explicit stipulations of the modes of valuing some assets have been made in the publicity laws of some jurisdictions. In 1948, the English legislation required that the market values of listed securities be given in the financial statements, by note if not otherwise. The same requirement has been adopted since in some other jurisdictions. An amendment of the English Act in 1967 required that, where assets were revalued, subsequent reports should show the dates, amounts and sources of the newer valuations. This does not secure that contemporary prices would be used, either for all assets or in any given year. But the dating, at least, provides some basis on which users can judge how out-of-date the figures are. It seems reasonable to suppose that the requirement contemplates that up-to-date prices yield functional information. Amendments to some Australian statutes in 1964

[8] Thomas H. Sanders, "Accounting Aspects of the Securities Act," *Law and Contemporary Problems*, IV (April 1937), p. 195.

required up-to-date valuations to be given for any real property to be charged as collateral security for any issue of senior securities.

## IV.  Functional Information—Particulars

Men frame their actions or choices on the basis of their general goals, their expectations and their present states. Of the three, the last is dominant. Knowledge of a present state may influence the goals that will be sought and the expectations that will be entertained. But neither goals nor expectations can influence a present state.

Though we have spoken of a present financial state in a general way with reference to market prices, it is made up of particulars, and it is analyzed by managers and others who combine those particulars in various ways. Let us say that there are at least three such combinations which are of interest—a measure of solvency such as the current ratio, a measure of debt to equity, and a measure of the rate of return or net income to residual equity. The numerators and denominators of these three ratios constitute six combinations of the particular components of a set of financial statements, and between them embrace all the usual components. The former two ratios may be of special interest to creditors, the latter two of interest to stockholders; and because F is smaller than W and more dependent on W than W is on F, F(M) will be concerned with all three. Knowing these ratios at a given date, F(M) may specify the state of F which is preferred at some future date; knowing what means are available at a given date, F(M) may specify, in general, by what steps the preferred future state may be reached; and knowing the change of state from some past date to the present date, F(M) may form some idea of what future change can be expected or should be expected. Of course, none of these particular bits of knowledge is functional unless in terms of contemporary resale prices.

We might, therefore, expect to find that accounting is done on a contemporary price basis. As we do not find this, we would expect to find that if the kinds of relationship we mention are used or discussed, there will be critical observations on the products of the kind of accounting in present use. Or, we would expect to find knowledgeable discussions of the affairs of firms which clearly entail or require the use of contemporary resale prices, even though they make no reference to accounting.

*The Evidence*

1. First, there are some accountants who doubt that the users of financial statements take any notice of the contents of balance sheets; perhaps this is rationalization of the inadequacy (known to accountants) of balance sheets to give the kinds of contemporary figures we stipulate. But, if analysts make reference to the use of balance sheet figures, we will have settled the question of what users use. Dun and Bradstreet and Robert Morris Associates have for some years published tabulations of some fourteen ratios for an extensive range of companies and industries.[9] The three types of ratios we mentioned appear in these series.

2. As the "source material" of analysis is not of the ideal kind, we expect to find suggestions of the manner in which the source material may be adjusted. We do.

    (a) "At the end of 1960 Bishop Oil Company owned 88,000 shares of Flintkote Corporation . . . carried at cost of $164,000 but worth $2,550,000 at market. For analytical purposes these shares should be considered as current assets at their market value less capital-gain tax on the indicated profit."[10]

    (b) "In December 1960 Kaiser Industries showed investments in Affiliated Companies of $182 million with a footnote indicating that their market value was $388 million. This market appreciation of $206 million is relevant to an analysis of Kaiser Industries shares."[11]

    (c) Commenting on two companies which reported the insured values of buildings and machinery at figures vastly greater than reported book values: "If figures such as these were required to be supplied by all companies as a footnote to the balance sheet a much more informative picture of the plant account would be available to [stockholders]."[12] The practice

---

[9] See *Annual Statement Studies*, The Staff of Robert Morris Associates; and of a different kind, R. A. Foulke, *Practical Financial Statement Analysis*, Third Edition (New York: McGraw-Hill Book Co., 1961).

[10] Benjamin Graham, David L. Dodd and Sidney Cottle, *Security Analysis: Principles and Technique*, Fourth Edition (New York: McGraw-Hill Book Company, Inc., 1962), p. 206.

[11] *Ibid.*, p. 207.

[12] *Ibid.*, p. 208.

here mentioned is also followed in some European countries. It has also been used and recommended for use in estimating national wealth and income.[13]

(d) In "The Missing Link in Supervision of the Securities Market,"[14] I cited a sample of comments of English financial statement analysts in the professional periodicals on the inadequacy of reported book values as bases for investors' judgments and the need for information more closely related to present market values.

3. Related to this kind of evidence is the view long held among some accountants that, if investors wish to have more up-to-date information they may go back over past reports, find when the assets were purchased and make their own estimations of what the present prices of assets might be. In an English case, *Re Press Caps Ltd* (1949), it seems likely that such a view was expressed in expert evidence or, if not, was expressed from the bench. The suggestion does not deny, implicitly it admits, the functional character of up-to-date information. But, the impossibility of an investor doing what is suggested is glossed over.

4. In jurisdictions in which the practice is not legally barred, occasional upward revaluation of assets is quite common. In view of the doctrine that cost is the proper basis for fixed asset accounting (a doctrine taught and said to be held by practitioners in those countries), this practice is anomalous. It is explicable only in terms of the inadequacy of the products of traditional accounting, and the resulting distortions of the ratios named at the beginning of this section. In a study of Australian listed companies for the ten years 1948–57, some 288 cases were found of stock dividends made from the "proceeds" of asset revaluations.[15] A subsequent study of Australian and New Zealand companies by McKee and Clarke, for the ten years ended June 1960, showed that 60 percent of the companies which continued through the decade had revalued

---

[13] See *Measuring the Nation's Wealth* (New York: Columbia University Press, 1964), p. 334. Papers from the Wealth Inventory Planning Study, George Washington University, National Bureau of Economic Research.

[14] R. J. Chambers, "The Missing Link in Supervision of the Securities Market," *Abacus*, V (September 1969), p. 16.

[15] Chambers, *A.F.M.*, pp. 107 ff.

assets at least once.[16] The practice has continued. It has been extensively followed also in England, and, I believe, in a number of other countries.

5.  In jurisdictions in which the practice of revaluing assets upwards is barred, it might be expected that there would be other evidence of the inconsistency between actual asset prices and book values, if the pressure of commercial circumstance can be relied upon to flush out such inconsistencies. The only evidence I know of at present is indirect. Undervaluation is permissible, gross undervaluation is permissible. Where commercial circumstance makes it desirable, the amount of undervaluation can be reduced (e.g., by varying the depreciation or inventory valuation method). But, being corseted by a law believed to limit valuations to cost, the system cannot directly disclose the extent of the discrepancy between book values and the current prices of assets. The only counter to this is to use supplementary statements, which have been suggested and have occasionally been used. This is an obviously weak line of evidence; but it is some evidence.

6.  A stronger line is given by the nature of mutual funds and unit trusts. These operate on the principle that contributors may generally withdraw at a price determined by the market prices of the assets. There seems to be no difference in principle between this kind and any other kind of investment *qua* investment. But, if it is not possible to allow stockholders of industrial corporations to withdraw from the corporation in exactly the same way, there seems to be every reason why they should be able to withdraw (by sale of their securities on the market) with the same kind of knowledge of what the underlying assets are currently worth at market resale prices.

7.  This last observation comes close to one of the possibilities available to creditors of and stockholders of companies. They have the nominal right to resolve to liquidate a company, creditors subject to constraints, stockholders without constraints. It is of no consequence that this is a nominal right, nor that stockholders seldom exercise it. If there is such a right, it entails that information shall be available which will enable stockholders to decide whether

---

[16] Chambers, *A.F.M.*, p. 194.

to liquidate a company if ever they should want so to decide. If assets are stated in amounts higher than resale prices, they would be misled as to the possible scale of alternative investments if they ever consider the liquidation possibility. If assets are stated in amounts lower than resale prices, they would also be misled, but in the opposite direction. In the first case, they would suppose a larger scale alternative than is possible, in the second, a smaller scale than is possible. The evidential point is simply the existence in law of the right to consider the alternative of liquidation. As for the managerial side of the matter, it is desired to avoid liquidation (in deference to the wishes or rights of any party whatsoever), the only way to avoid it is to keep constantly under observation the facts which are indicative of solvency—the relationships of debts to assets at market prices. A recent and apposite example of the relevance of market prices will be found in the report of the judgment in the Court of Appeals in the Continental Vending case.[17]

8. We have noticed the independently stated views of some analysts. We may notice the independently stated views of some economists. Analysis of the opportunities available to firms (in microeconomic theory) begins with the supposition that the firm is financially able to operate through the whole range of outputs contemplated in the examples used; in short, it has the money (or money and goods whose resale prices will make good the deficiency in money). The comparison of alternative courses thus proceeds from a known present state. Point one. Point two. Those writers who make reference to that state specify it by reference to resale prices. The discussion is sometimes related to income, that is, the difference between two states.

(a) "Personal income may be defined as the algebraic sum of (1) the market value of rights exercised in consumption and (2) the change in the store of property of rights between the beginning and end of the period in question . . . measured . . . by appeal to market prices . . . [or] according to objective market standards."[18]

[17] See "Continental Vending Decision Affirmed," *The Journal of Accountancy*, CXXIX (February 1970), p. 61.

[18] H. C. Simons, *Personal Income Taxation* (Chicago: University of Chicago Press, 1938), p. 50.

(b) The definition of income *ex post* "which is the most important" of three possible definitions is that it "equals the value of the individual's consumption plus the increment in the money value of his prospect which has accrued during the week; it equals consumption plus capital accumulation . . . it is an objective magnitude . . . [involving] a comparison between present values and values which belong wholly to the past."[19]

(c) Edwards and Bell make a stronger case for opportunity cost valuation (resale prices) than any other of the alternatives they considered.[20] The reason why they did not adopt it seems to be in the position taken that opportunity cost valuation relates to complete liquidation as an alternative, whereas the liquidation of any asset at any time is just as feasible an alternative, and indeed a more common one.

(d) Perhaps plainer than any form of verbal description is the example given in Lipsey and Steiner's *Economics*.[21] With the object of distinguishing the conventional accounting procedure from the procedure entailed in the mode of economic analysis, they set up the accounts of an imaginary firm on both bases. The "economist's balance sheet" is there shown quite clearly to be based on market prices at opening and closing dates, the depreciation is shown as the difference between two market prices, and the income of the period as the difference between the opening and closing values of the net equity calculated in that way.

## V. *Functional Information—Comparison*

Choosing between two or more possibilities is the easier if one or more properties common to the possibilities can be measured in a common scale. Assessing the relative performances and other features of two or more entities engaged in different activities is made easier

[19] J. R. Hicks, *Value and Capital: An Inquiry into Some Fundamental Principles of Economic Theory*, Second Edition (London: Oxford University Press, 1939), pp. 178–9.

[20] Edgar O. Edwards and Philip W. Bell, *The Theory and Measurement of Business Income* (Berkeley, California: University of California Press, 1961), pp. 80 ff.

[21] Richard G. Lipsey and Peter O. Steiner, *Economics* (New York: Harper & Row Publishers, 1966), p. 207.

if one or more of the characteristics of those entities can be measured in a common scale. It is commonly claimed that the publication of accounts provides the basis on which comparisons may be made of the financial properties of companies. Some do not readily admit this, but these simply fly in the face of the necessities and practices of men.

The object of any measurement scheme is to supply measured magnitudes which may be used in a wide variety of contexts—by one user in many kinds of calculations, or by many users each in his own calculations. Any balance sheet or income figure which is derived by a combination of rules unique to its issuer is, at best, limited in use to those who "derived" it. For they alone know how it was derived. But, typically, those who derive the figures do not use them. In the terms we employed earlier, the products of F(A) are used by F(M). If F(M) wishes to compare F with any other firm in W, F(M) can perhaps ask F(A) to what extent the products of F(A) should be adjusted to make them comparable. But this is not fruitful, for any other firm G in W may also have unique products of its G(A), the effects of which cannot be discovered by F(A).

Comparisons of the states and the rates of change of state of two or more firms are impossible unless the component items are expressed in the same (contemporary) terms, both as to the units used and as to the prices expressed in those units (and, in particular, as to the use of resale prices, since they alone express elements of the claims of firms as against the rest of the community).

We would expect either that such a form of accounting is used; or that there would be expressions of objection and attempts at correction on the part of those who must use the products of the system of accounting that is used; or that there would be evidence of losses falling unexpectedly on those who rely on published figures which are not comparable.

*The Evidence*

1. First, the point that comparisons *are* necessary to some parties of interest. Information services associated with the securities markets publish extensive tabulations of figures drawn from and based on financial statements. *Standard NYSE Stock Reports*, for example, gives up to ten years statistics of income, balance sheet figures and security prices, including such deduced figures as the current ratio

and the book value of common stock. We have already mentioned the Dun and Bradstreet and Robert Morris Associates compilations. The latter give the median and upper and lower quartile values of the ratios they compute for each industry in their systems. This type of calculation is technically meaningless if the component figures are not of the same kind (i.e., if they are derived by rules unique to each company). All of these services would be meaningless unless it were expected (and confirmed by the sale of the services) that comparisons would be and are made in forming judgments on securities.

2.  Those parts of the literatures of accounting and security analysis which deal with financial statement analysis commonly contain warnings about making direct comparisons of different companies, because of the different rules available generally to each and all companies. If comparison were not a natural or legitimate response to the appearance of financial statements, there would be no occasion for the warnings and the elaborate descriptions of the differences which different ways of accounting yield.

3.  The use of common words and the whole case for standardizing terminology rests on the supposition that the amounts corresponding with the verbal notations are similar in kind and, therefore, comparable. If it were not so, we should find an elaborate description of the particulars represented. Instead of just "net income," we should find "net income—FIFO—SYD—GA—TA—variety," for example (meaning FIFO inventory; sum of year's digits depreciation; goodwill amortization; tax allocation), and many similar or fancier varieties. In the absence of this kind of full disclosure, it can only be supposed that accountants intend that the figures should be compared. (This may seem at odds with the point of the previous paragraph, but such oddities are to be expected when the product does not meet all of its tests simultaneously.)

4.  Arguments for common dollar accounting are all partially in contemplation of the comparison of the resulting figures, whether or not the common dollars are "contemporary" dollars (a condition of interpretability, already mentioned) or dollars of any other specified date. All such arguments are, in effect, criticisms of the adequacy of the prevailing mode of accounting.

5. The problem of comparison is particularly of concern to regulatory and concession-granting agencies which administer particular trades or classes of trade or terms of trade, where comparisons of particular firms or aggregations of characteristics of classes of firms must be made. As two recent examples:

(a) In June 1969, *The Journal of Accountancy* noted a revision of the regulations of the Small Business Administration, requiring that Small Business Investment Companies shall report "unrealized appreciation of assets" of each concern which the Small Business Investment Company has helped to finance. The amount would be the difference between "total assets as recorded in the small business concern's books" and "total assets based on their estimated market value or fair value as of the close of the fiscal year."[22]

(b) In December 1969, *The Journal of Accountancy* reported on a Federal Trade Commission study which said that existing accounting practices "have granted merger-minded companies almost limitless opportunity to understate the market value of investments in acquired enterprises." Calling for the elimination of pooling of interests accounting, the study said: "Insofar as possible, every merger transaction should be accounted for in a way that will most accurately represent the true value of the individual assets acquired."[23]

6. Comparison of the financial characteristics of companies is one element in the decision to merge or not, to sell one's shareholding to a takeover bidder at one price or another, and all similar decisions. Many bids are clearly in contemplation of acquiring the the assets of a company at a lower price than they could otherwise be acquired. There may, in some cases, be other expectations also, but these will simply be "causes" of the extent to which the bidder is prepared to bid *above* the prices at which the assets could be acquired. Where a bid is by way of an exchange of shares, the *ostensible* comparison is of the market prices of the shares. The

[22] "SBA Revises Reporting Requirements for SBICs," *The Journal of Accountancy*, CXXVII (June 1969), p. 20.
[23] "FTC Study Urges Elimination of Pooling of Interests," *The Journal of Accountancy*, CXXVIII (December 1969), p. 12.

underlying comparison of the bidder is of what he has to pay (the market price of the shares offered) with what he expects to get. If the assets of an offeree company are understated by comparison with their contemporary market prices, the extent of the past gains of the company will also have been understated. On one ground or the other, the shares will tend to be priced in the market at less than the price could be if the actual extent of the gains and the net assets had been disclosed, hence, the opportunity of the bidder, through the ignorance of the shareholder of the offeree company.

(a) Loss cites an action brought successfully against Transamerica Corporation which turned on an undervaluation of the tobacco inventory of Axton-Fisher Tobacco Company, which Transamerica had acquired. The action was based on Rule 10b-5 under the Securities Exchange Act of 1934, relating to insider trading to the detriment of uninformed public security holders. Commenting on the case and the judgment, Loss observes: "It is no answer that accounting practice normally favors the carrying of assets at cost or market, whichever is *lower*, so as to present a conservative rather than a roseate view of the company's affairs. The cost-or-market-whichever-is-lower formula operates in quite the reverse manner, of course, when the company is *buying* rather than *selling* its securities. Nor is it an answer that the Commission's accounting rules do not specifically require inventory to be priced at market value. For Regulation S-X does provide that the specified information shall be furnished 'as a minimum requirement to which shall be added such further material information as is necessary to make the required statements . . . not misleading.' "[24]

(b) Elsewhere I have shown that from a selection of Australian takeovers, share prices can rise by over 100 percent on the announcement of a bid. I interpret this as the reaction of the market to new information (the offer), indicative, at least to some extent, of asset values in excess of reported values.[25] There are also cases in which asset revaluation has been

[24] Louis Loss, *Securities Regulation*, Second Edition, Vol. III (Boston: Little, Brown and Co., 1961), pp. 1058–62. Footnotes omitted.
[25] Chambers, *A.F.M.*, pp. 191–3.

explicitly described as a defense against takeovers.[26] Shareholders who bought or sold prior to the announcements of bids clearly did not know what they were buying or selling. The unexpected "losses" of some (through unsuspected ignorance) yielded unexpected gains to others.

(c)  There are numerous cases where bidders have been able to acquire substantial properties, without or nearly without cost, through purchasing securities and meeting the purchase price out of disposal of only part of the assets which came under their control. One Australian company thus acquired an airline, liquidating the airline company's investment portfolio for the cost of the airline securities purchased. Examples of English cases are given in Bull and Vice, *Bid for Power*,[27] and Marriott, *The Property Boom*.[28] No doubt there are many such cases in the U.S. Their success depends on knowledge of asset values which bidders are able to acquire by search, but of which stockholders are kept in ignorance.

7.  There are, on the other hand, examples of companies whose shareholders and creditors have sustained substantial losses through belief in financial statements which represented at cost assets which had or came to have much lower market prices than their costs. Some Australian examples are given in *A.F.M.*[29]

8.  On numerous occasions, members and officials of the SEC have stressed the importance of the comparability of the information yielded by accounting and made available to the public. There would be no occasion for the stress were it not that comparison is necessary to choice and that the present forms of accounting do not permit proper comparisons.

### Conclusion

The bits of evidence cited are only examples of larger masses of evidence in the same direction under each of the heads mentioned. It

---

[26] Chambers, *A.F.M.*, p. 111.

[27] George Bull and Anthony Vice, *Bid for Power*, Third Edition (London: Elek Books, Ltd., 1961).

[28] Oliver Marriott, *The Property Boom* (London: Hamish, Hamilton, Ltd., 1967).

[29] Chambers, *A.F.M.*, pp. 204 ff.

is emphasized that all of this evidence is observational; it relates to events which do or did occur; none of it is manufactured or hypothetical. It all points to the functional property of contemporary information and, in particular, to the functional significance of market resale prices. It tends to the confirmation of the conclusions which may be reached, on empirico-logical grounds, in respect of the functional character of the products of a system of accounting on the basis of market selling prices.

The variety and weight of this evidence may be set against the variety and weight of similar evidence for any other system of accounting. Let it be remembered that the argument given in the introduction recognizes the necessity of present value *calculations*, as and when necessary, but such calculations depend on knowledge of present market prices of assets and present states. Let it be remembered that initial prices are necessary inputs of a market price system, but the latter does not arbitrarily exclude the effects of subsequent changes in prices; the system we here support is more completely historical than historical cost accounting. Let it be remembered that continuously contemporary accounting takes account of the differential effects of changes in prices and changes in price levels, whereas this differential is disregarded in price level adjusted historical cost accounting. Let it be remembered that an entry (or replacement) price system does not yield information indicative of the present state of a firm in its relations with the rest of the world. On all these grounds, it seems extremely unlikely that the quantity of independent evidence for any other system can approach the evidence for a market-selling price system. The supporters of other systems are invited to attempt to match it.

At least until contrary evidence is tendered, we conclude that a market-selling price accounting system is a functional part of a well-designed business system.

# Response to
# Evidence for a Market—Selling Price—
# Accounting System

*by* FRANK T. WESTON

ARTHUR YOUNG & COMPANY

PROFESSOR CHAMBERS has submitted some very interesting evidence. However, I have the impression that, upon further scrutiny, some of his evidence may not support the market-selling price accounting system which he recommends.

In order to put the subject of Professor Chambers' paper into proper perspective, I would like to focus on the subject matter of this symposium—"Asset Valuation and Income Determination: A Consideration of the Alternatives." In stressing the topic under discussion and in assessing Professor Chambers' treatment of it, I may, I am afraid, anticipate some of the discussion scheduled later. However, this approach enables me to compare the advantages and disadvantages of Professor Chambers' accounting system with some of the others in particular areas.

In discussing asset valuation and income determination, it seems clear that the major emphasis today is on the determination of income. The widespread interest in investment opportunities and in the comparative yields of competing investments means that a great number of individuals and institutions are concerned with one product of the accounting system: net income. Therefore, it seems to me that we are looking for a system of asset valuation which will give us the most meaningful, and therefore the most useful, measure of income for a period.

In this connection, I am reminded of the definition of income which

Professor Sidney Davidson often offers for our consideration: "Income is the measure of how much better off the entity is at December 31st as compared with January 1st." In a real, economic sense, this is certainly an accurate definition. This definition would doubtless lead us to some sort of current value system for measuring all assets and liabilities. As I will point out later, this definition would not necessarily lead us to the market-selling price system which Professor Chambers supports. Furthermore, the current value approach would not appear to be relevant to many of the decisions which management and investors are currently making about an entity. At the risk of pre-judging our conclusions, I would suggest that no one system of asset valuation and income measurement will do the job properly.

Let us examine the relevance of market-selling price information to the two groups which have overriding interests in asset valuation and income measurement—management and investors.

In a few cases, market-selling price data are clearly relevant. The best example is a mutual fund—a regulated investment company continuously offering its shares to the public and continually redeeming shares offered by its shareholders. In this situation, investors are buying and selling shares based on the current market prices of the underlying investment portfolio. The aggregate of the current market prices of the underlying securities is the *only* measurement which is of concern to them. These investors are involved in a continuous process of comparing yield with market levels. In this trading environment, yield on market and changes in market are essential information. These investors truly know how much better off they are today compared with last year, or last month, or last week. They are interested almost exclusively in asset selling prices. It seems to me that this is one of the few logical and necessary applications of Professor Chambers' accounting system.

Another such situation would be a company in liquidation. As contrasted with the continuous buying and selling activities of mutual funds, this is an example of the final, one-time sale of assets. In this situation, market-selling price information is also the only meaningful data.

In connection with the importance of market price data in a situation involving liquidation or disposition of assets, a recent court proceeding generated some very interesting reading.[1] The case involved the merger of two companies. Management of the acquiring company had apparently decided that, following the merger, it would attempt to dispose of a substantial portion of the assets of the acquired business. There was apparently little doubt that disposal of these assets would result in a substantial gain. Neither the possibility of such sales nor the potential resulting gain was apparently disclosed in the proxy statement used to solicit proxies from the minority stockholders of the company being acquired. These stockholders later took the position that they should have been advised of the intended disposition of the assets of their company and of their estimated sales value. The Securities and Exchange Commission entered the case and filed an *amicus curiae* brief, discussing various aspects of disclosure of current values. Since the SEC is an agency which has strenuously objected to the introduction of current value data into financial statements, its brief makes interesting reading. While the SEC did not suggest that the data as to estimated fair values be included in the financial statements, it did take the position that, in these particular circumstances, good faith offers and reliable appraisals must be disclosed if their omission would render the proxy statement materially misleading. The court agreed with that position and concluded that the proxy statement was misleading. I am sure Professor Chambers will be interested in this evidence as to a situation in which market-selling price data are considered relevant.

A third situation in which market-selling price information might be relevant is that involving a passive, long-term investment in an asset which represents a major portion of the resources of an entity. An example would be an entity holding antiques or land for long-term appreciation. Certain long-term investment situations might also be included. In these cases, investors buying and selling securities in such entities would certainly be in favor of an accounting system which indicates market-selling prices as relevant information. Here again, the economic activities of the entity revolve around the resale of the assets in their present form. Thus, data as to market prices are most meaningful.

In many other situations, market-selling price information is clearly not relevant. It seems to me that the life insurance industry is a good

---

[1] *Gerstle v. Gamble-Skogmo, Inc.* (298 F. Supp. 66, EDNY 1969).

example of this type of case. Here is an industry which is basically involved in long-term contractual arrangements under which two principal factors—yield on investments and mortality experience—determine economic results for the entity. The "operating cycle" of such an industry—at least in terms of whole life policies—is long-term. These companies are, in effect, matching over a long term (1) their actual investment yields with those yields assumed for policy and reserve computations, and (2) their actual mortality experience with the mortality experience assumed for policy and reserve computations. Under these conditions, a measurement of income, to be reasonably accurate, must be based on a long period of time. How much better off such a company is between the beginning of one year and the end of that year is really not relevant to investment decisions in that industry. The long-term investments in corporate bonds or in mortgages are acquired with the intention to hold them until maturity. Under normal conditions, fluctuations in the market prices of such investments are not relevant to the determination of income of a life insurance company, since it does not intend to liquidate these investments at the particular year-end. However, accounting attempts to furnish information for relatively short, annual periods for the use of investors. It would appear that investors in such an industry must learn more about the operating cycle of these specialized situations. Then, with the relevant, long-term information available, they can, hopefully, make better investment decisions.

Leaving those situations in which market-selling price information is clearly relevant or clearly irrelevant, let us turn our attention to the typical manufacturing or service company. Here we find a strange mixture of relevancy and irrelevancy with respect to current market information.

Regarding the typical manufacturing or service company, it seems to me that the investor—and management as well—wants to know the answers to five questions:

(1) How much better off is his company at the end of the year, compared with its status at the beginning of the year?

(2) How did his company achieve this? That is, what did its management do, how did they do it, what are the significant aspects of performance?

(3) How does the performance of his company compare with that of other companies?

(4) How will his company do in the future?

(5) How will all this affect his own investment yield?

It seems to me that our accounting system today tries to answer all these questions for management and for the investor. My own view is that our present system—or indeed any other single system—cannot adequately answer these five questions.

But, let us move on to assess Professor Chambers' market-selling price system of valuation in terms of how well it furnishes answers to these five questions.

As to how much better off the company is at the end of the year, I would agree that the market-selling price system does give accurate information as to how much better off the company is, *if* we are dealing in economic theory or *if* it actually plans to sell its assets at year-end. But, such information is relevant to the investor only if the management does, in fact, plan to liquidate and sell its assets. If the company plans instead to continue its normal manufacturing and service activities, then that information is totally irrelevant for almost all parties. (I would agree that management might use such information in considering a decision to liquidate at year-end, but it does not seem realistic to assume that the management of every company makes such a decision on a continual basis. In a world perfectly in balance economically, this should happen; in the real world, it probably does not happen often enough to warrant the preparation of otherwise irrelevant accounting information as the primary published data.)

As for the second question—how did the company achieve its progress or lack of progress during the year—the market-selling price system does not seem to help at all. The income statement proposed by Professor Chambers shows one amount for revenues (sales), followed by an amount for cost of sales, which is the same amount as revenues, since prices of inventories are adjusted continuously to market prices. Thus, "gross profit" is zero. Further down in the statement there is an amount called "price adjustment." This contains all manner of fluctuations in prices, holding gains, manufacturing efficiencies, etc. To be useful to any reader, the income statement must be expanded to include a detailed analysis of the price adjustment amount. Based on suggested income statements in this format, this system does not do a good job of showing how the company moved from its economic status at the beginning of the year to its status at the end of the year.

With this background, we might conclude that the historical cost system—properly adjusted to remove the effects of general price level changes—does the best job of demonstrating how the company got from one year-end to another: what its sales were, what its manufacturing costs were, how much it produced, what its general and selling costs were, what various significant ratios were for the year and at both year-ends. That system does furnish relevant information of a truly historical nature. The replacement cost system will not do so. None of the market price systems will do so.

The third question—how does the performance of one company compare with that of other companies—is one of the most important in our investor-oriented world today. All the accounting systems under review appear to fail in this area. The market-selling price system seems to offer little help, since the important comparative data are apparently buried in the "price adjustments" caption. This system, by placing major emphasis on *price* changes—and very little emphasis on purchase, manufacturing and selling efficiencies—appears to offer little useful information for this purpose. The discounted cash flow system also appears to be unsatisfactory. By discounting all future cash flows and, presumably, using the excess of cash inflows over outflows to determine the "value" of the operating property, plant and equipment, this method appears to "bury" labor inefficiencies in the reduced valuation of the fixed assets. Thus, as between two companies which are identical in all respects except for the efficiency of the labor forces, if the same discount rate were used, the one with the efficient labor force would presumably have a higher "value" for its plant than the inefficient one, and the only apparent indication of this situation would be that the plant of the inefficient producer would be carried at a lower value. Use of the discounted cash flow system for an entire business—as opposed to a capital investment decision—needs further study.

On the other hand, the historical cost system does not adequately disclose how the performance of one company compares with that of another. The adequacy of such comparisons depends, as we know, on whether the two companies acquired their plants at about the same time—in terms of basic cost, subsequent general price level changes, etc.

Of all the systems under review, the replacement cost system probably furnishes the best answer to the question of comparative performance. This system, being based on third party cost data, would highlight labor inefficiencies as between two companies.

As for another critical question for investors—how will the company do in the future—the market-selling price system is of little help. The discounted cash flow system also seems to fail. I must confess that the historical cost system and the replacement cost system do not seem to have the proper answer either. There is a possibility that replacement cost information, together with historical cost data, could give the investor the maximum information which any past-transaction oriented system could provide.

For example, assume that a manufacturing company with a plant constructed in 1940 is competing with an identical company with a plant constructed in 1960. Assuming that other variable factors are truly comparable, the income statements of these two companies differ primarily due to the different amounts of depreciation. Based on the historical cost method, the 1940 company appears to be doing a better job than the 1960 company. However, if the investor knew that, in three years, the 1940 company would have to replace its plant and incur depreciation charges based on 1972 costs, he would have some very relevant information. The fact that such information is not now supplied seems to be the principal weakness of the historical cost system. But, suppose that the financial statements were to disclose the imminence of replacement and the estimated increased depreciation costs which are anticipated? Then we appear to have the best of the accounting systems in terms of relevant information for investors. Managements presumably already have such information.

Now, for the last question—how will all this affect the yield of the investor? Now we have a veritable Alice in Wonderland! What, if any, correlation is there between the "income" of a company and the "yield" to an investor in that company? This question has application to both short-term and long-term investments. For this purpose, I am sure that we can agree that "yield" represents the return—either in the form of dividends or eventual capital gains—on an investment in securities of a company. Then we come to a very important question—given a particular method of determining income for the corporate entity, will there be any relationship between the results of such a determination and the actual yield to the investor? If there is such a relationship, how does the average investor determine it? If there is no such relationship, how does the average investor make his decisions?

We know that in recent years, corporations have paid dividends which amounted, on the average, to approximately 50% of net income. Thus, the current yield, in terms of dividends, can be fairly well correlated with reported income. But, will present dividend payout ratios remain constant, or will they increase or decrease? Furthermore, what about the other facet of yield—capital gains? Is there any basis for believing that the reinvestment of a portion of current earnings will necessarily result in higher future earnings, with higher absolute per share dividend payouts and resulting higher market prices for the common shares? At this point, all the accounting systems seem to disappoint—as well they might, since we are now engaged in forecasting in an area affected by countless variables.

However, should not the investor be educated to consider the possible correlation between the company's net income and his yield? It seems to me that the experience of investors with the shares of holding companies with savings and loan association subsidiaries is a good example of this problem. Until the income tax laws were changed a few years ago, there was little possibility that these companies could pay any cash dividends, since the earnings of the underlying associations were "frozen" in their general reserves and could not be paid to the parent company. Nevertheless, the reported earnings of these holding companies received favorable reaction from investors, and there was somewhat of a "boom" in these shares. It is difficult to imagine how investors could be attracted to such investments—short of liquidation, no dividends would be forthcoming. On the other hand, build-up of values, sheltered in these reserves, did occur. However, unless one adopts the cynical approach of the "chain letter" philosophy (there will, hopefully, always be someone else to whom an investor can sell his shares at a higher price), there appears to be little justification for the investor interest in such shares. This is, in my view, a classic example of the wide disparity between a company's net income and an investor's yield. (As an aside, possibly investors have finally come to appreciate this distinction—the shares of these holding companies have declined in popularity in recent years, even in spite of a change in the tax law, which effectively permits payments of limited amounts of dividends up to the parent holding company. Many other factors have, of course, also affected the market value of such shares.

I suppose my conclusion on this question is that a well-informed investor should be able to understand any one of the accounting systems under review, and, understanding them, to form his own conclusions as to any correlation of net income and yield. Here is another area which needs extended research.

In summary, viewed in the light of the five critical tests, I have come to the conclusion that Professor Chambers' market-selling price accounting system does not stand up. It simply does not furnish information relevant for management or investors.

It seems to me that the historical cost system—adjusted to eliminate the effects of general price level increases—provides useful information about most of the activities of the typical manufacturing or service company. Supplemental data from the other accounting systems is essential in certain circumstances.

In closing, I would like to leave one suggestion as to how accounting and accountants can furnish—or help to furnish—certain additional information which would be very helpful to investors. This is the suggestion which a small *ad hoc* committee of the AICPA discussed with Commissioner Francis M. Wheat in the course of the study of disclosures undertaken recently by the SEC. We indicated to Commissioner Wheat that a very practical means of overcoming or reducing the impact of some of the weaknesses of historical cost accounting—and, in fact, of any other system of accounting which could reasonably be implemented—would be to require the furnishing of *budget information* in annual reports to stockholders. This would bridge some of the gap between historical cost accounting and replacement cost accounting, and would also introduce some formality into answering the most important question which investors ask of corporate management—how will my company do in the future?

You will be interested to know that Commissioner Wheat was intrigued by this suggestion. A small section in the final "Wheat Report" discusses this subject but concludes that the present SEC policy of prohibiting earnings forecasts should not be changed. However, it seems to me that the investor can properly ask for two bits of information from management and its accountants: How did we *really* do last year? and How do you estimate we will do next year? As accountants we should strive to answer both questions effectively.

## 5

# Asset Valuation and Income Determination: Appraising the Alternatives

*by* DAVID SOLOMONS

UNIVERSITY OF PENNSYLVANIA

BEFORE alternative accounting methods can be appraised, there has to be some agreement as to the criteria by which they are to be judged. There surely can be no dispute that the overriding criterion must be relevance. The secondary criterion is feasibility. I define "feasibility" to include all the other qualities which make a measurement method acceptable as a practical tool. Thus, feasibility includes objectivity, low cost of implementation, and ease of understanding by those for whose benefit it is being used. If a measurement method fails to meet any of these tests, then it will not do. Unfortunately, these criteria do not provide us with a go/no-go test, for almost any reasonable accounting method will satisfy both criteria to some extent. Each method will give us a different mix of qualities. Historical cost, for example, gives us a high degree of feasibility but rather little relevance. The other methods give us more relevance and somewhat less feasibility, in varying proportions.

One of the interesting points that emerges from most of the papers, it seems to me, is that the doubts which have so often been expressed about the feasibility of the alternatives to historical cost are not nearly as serious as they are usually thought to be, especially if we take the computer into account. Philip Bell, in his paper, has referred to the successful testing of the use of replacement costs by Peter Dickerson in California.[1] The use of the exit values has also been successfully tested by James McKeown at Michigan State University.[2] As Staubus explains in his paper, cash flows, where they are used, are usually represented in accounts by a surrogate, either net realizable value or replacement cost. The problems of implementing the alternatives to historical cost are, therefore, not insoluble nor excessively costly. This seems to leave the ground clear for a battle over the issue of relevance. In any case, the cost of obtaining information can hardly be usefully discussed without regard to the value of the information which results. Perhaps it is true, in accounting as elsewhere, that you get what you pay for.

While I am full of admiration for Ijiri's skillful defense of historical cost accounting, he does not persuade me that we would be wise to give up the attempt to replace it with something better. He makes a good deal of what he calls "chaining inputs and outputs." But I doubt whether historical cost necessarily gives us a good measure either of inputs or outputs. When inputs are used immediately, or almost immediately, upon acquisition, purchase cost and input are more or less identical, so that historical cost will satisfactorily measure input. But, if there is a time lag between acquisition and use, this identity is lost. We then have an input bearing an out-of-date price tag, which may masquerade as a current input without really having any right to do so. As for outputs, I cannot see that historical cost accounting can claim to measure these in value terms at all, unless the identification of outputs with inputs can be described as output measurement. To do so is to confuse cost and value, to adopt implicitly a Cost Theory of Value, which economists abandoned a century ago. The cost of an activity does not give it value; it is the value of the activity which justifies the incurrence of cost.

The identification of cost and value is not made more respectable by being ascribed to the working of the double-entry system, as Ijiri does. I do not believe, as he does, that this is the essence and the crowning achievement of double-entry. The essence of double-entry, I suggest, is that it introduces an account for proprietorship to

[1] Peter Dickerson, *Business Income—A Critical Analysis*, Institute of Business and Economic Research (Berkeley: University of California Press, 1965).

[2] James McKeown, *An Application of a Current-Market-Value Accounting Model* (Michigan State University, 1969, unpublished).

close the balance sheet equation. This is what distinguishes double-entry from single-entry bookkeeping. It could reflect current costs just as easily as historical costs in terms of double-entry records. Indeed, double-entry would be seen in full bloom, so to speak, if it were used to credit proprietorship with unrealized value changes.

When Ijiri claims that historical costs are additive, whereas current costs are not, he is really carrying the war into the enemy's camp. The fact is, I suggest, that historical costs are additive only in the sense that any set of numbers drawn from the same number system can be added together. The important question is whether the resulting aggregate has any significance. Surely, the significance of any aggregate of historical expenditures made at different dates, during a period in which prices have been fluctuating, must be quite dubious.

Ijiri makes a good deal of the supposed advantage that historical cost accounting uses actual transactions rather than hypothetical transactions. Too much can be made of this point. For one thing, even historical cost accounting makes use of hypothetical transactions sometimes, as when it values inventory at cost or market value, whichever is the lower. It also uses hypothetical transactions when it sets up standard costs, when it adds notes on the market value of assets such as securities, and when it calculates earnings per share on a fully diluted basis. But more importantly, information about actual transactions which took place at one date may be less relevant at another date than information about hypothetical transactions which might have taken place at that second date. And these hypothetical transactions are almost always transactions which have actually been entered into by somebody, even though the accounting entity itself was not a party to them.

When we come to the problems of aggregation and disaggregation that Ijiri discusses, it seems to me that the score is about even as between historical cost accounting and its alternatives. Different purchase prices for different-sized purchase lots can introduce anomalies into historical accounting records, even when we are dealing with actual transactions. The same material purchased in two different-sized lots on the same date might have to be recorded at different prices. I cannot see that the aggregation of these two actual transactions, just because they are "actual," has any more validity than if they were hypothetical. And I am reminded, at this point, that some defenders of standard costing, when that accounting development was in its infancy sixty years ago, argued that *standard* costs were truer costs than *actual* costs, because actual costs included the adventitious results of scrap, idle time and inefficiencies of various kinds and these were not "proper costs," to use John Whitmore's expression.[3]

To admit, as Ijiri does, that the problems of *disaggregation* occur only—I repeat his word "only"—"when resources purchased originally as a group are split among periods, departments, or products," (p. 7) is to admit quite a lot. It is just the need to allocate resources between periods that gives rise to all the problems of depreciation and inventory valuation which have caused such dissatisfaction with historical cost accounting.

It is true, as Ijiri claims, that much historical data is of great value for management. But let us remember that much of this useful information has little or nothing to do with historical costs. It relates to physical quantities or to the details of sales transactions. It is information of a kind which would be recorded, whatever methods of income measurement were used. And if information about historical costs were thought to be useful for managerial purposes, it could well be recorded and aggregated, whatever alternatives to historical cost accounting were used for other purposes.

At the other end of the spectrum, Ray Chambers is the champion of "exit" values. I find his espousal of market resale values much too sweeping for my taste. It is valuable to be reminded, as he does remind us, that there are many situations in which stockholders cannot be fully informed about the affairs of their companies unless they are given information about market values. But accepting the truth of that view does not require us to agree that *only* market values are relevant in accounting. The crucial test of the usefulness of exit values in accounting statements lies in the treatment of highly specific assets in a balance sheet. These assets may have very little value for anyone except the present owner for whom they were constructed. Certainly their market sale value may be much below cost. Yet, presumably, they were worth at least as much as they cost their owners when they were acquired, for otherwise they would not have been constructed or purchased. What sense would it make in accounting statements to write

[3] John Whitmore, "Shoe Factory Cost Accounts," *Journal of Accountancy* (May, 1908).

such assets down to their current resale value as soon as they were brought into use? The acquisition of these assets would have to be shown as involving their owners in a considerable loss of capital. This kind of accounting simply would not reflect the facts of the situation. Or at least it would reflect only one of the less important facts.

This brings me to a valuation concept which, I think, could do much to integrate many of the conflicting ideas which have been expressed at this meeting. It is Bonbright's concept of "value to the owner." "The value of a property to its owner," said Bonbright, "is identical in amount with the adverse value of the entire loss, direct and indirect, that the owner might expect to suffer if he were to be deprived of the property."[4] In general, for business assets, this loss will be equal to the discounted value of expected net receipts.

Expressed in this way, "value to the owner" would appear to be much too subjective a concept to be of use to the accountant. And so it would be if it could not be quantified objectively, at least within tolerably close limits. Fortunately, we can approximate it fairly well, if we note that it is bounded by net realizable value on the lower side and replacement cost on the upper side. It is clear that an asset cannot be worth less to its owner than he could sell it for. It is also clear that the loss which he would sustain, if he were deprived of an asset, cannot be greater than the cost to which he would be put to replace it or its services, if an alternative asset can provide them more cheaply. The relationships between these concepts have been sufficiently explored by Bell and Staubus in their papers, so that it is not necessary to dwell on them again. However, it does help in several ways to think of net realizable value and replacement cost as surrogates for value to the owner, for when we do, some of their properties fall into place. For example, George Staubus, it seems to me, is unduly worried in his paper about the additivity of net realizable values and of replacement costs. If we think of them both as surrogates for values to the owner, then when we add them together, we are simply adding together values to the owner. The resulting aggregate then takes on a clear and unique meaning.

Though it is fitting that the problem of additivity should receive careful attention, my experience as an academic suggests that it is

[4] James C. Bonbright, *The Valuation of Property*, Volume I (New York: McGraw-Hill, 1937), p. 71.

easy to be over-sensitive about it. Consider the process of giving a student a grade for a course. He receives a number of marks for examination performance. He gets some credit, perhaps, for class participation, some more for regularity in submitting homework. Perhaps his performance in playing a business game is also taken into account. Each kind of "performance" is a surrogate for what we are really trying to measure—his quality as a student. Somehow, by a process of aggregation, which would probably not survive too careful an investigation, a single grade is eventually awarded. The system seems to work.

If additivity is a source of difficulty, so also is the problem of complementarity. Fortunately, the upper limit to "value to the owner" set by replacement cost also enables us to resolve the difficult question of the relationship of the values of the parts of a complex business to the whole. The lack of one vital part of a machine could bring the whole machine to a standstill. Thus, the value of the part to the owner of the machine might be equated with the value of the whole machine. If we did this for each of several vital parts, we should finish up with an aggregate value for the machine equal to several times the value of the machine—a manifest absurdity. Fortunately, if each vital part can be replaced separately, its value to the owner will be limited to the cost of replacing *it*, not the whole machine; and these several replacement costs will approximate in total to— they will not add up to—the value to the owner of the whole machine.

For assets which are not held for resale, replacement cost is generally a better surrogate for value to the owner than is net realizable value. The fact that the asset is being held, not sold, may be taken to mean that if the owner were deprived of it, he would want to replace it, or at least its services, unless the expected net receipts are less than replacement cost. The sale value of an asset which is not going to be sold does not seem to be relevant in assessing the "well offness" of the asset's owner.

In defense of the use of market resale values for income determination purposes, Chambers, and Edwards and Bell also, equate these values with the opportunity cost of using assets. This easy identification of sale value and opportunity cost may not always be justified. The opportunity cost of using an asset is determined by its value in its next best alternative use. That is how opportunity cost is defined. The alternative to using an asset now is not necessarily to sell it; and, in fact, if for some reason an operating asset is forced to become idle for a short period, its owner will normally not put it on the market. He will retain it for use later. Except for rapidly obsolescing assets, the alternative to present use is generally future use, not realization. The total chronological life of the asset will be extended when it stands idle for a time. It will not generally be thrown onto the market. Thus, the opportunity cost of using an asset now is more generally determined by the loss of future cash flows resulting from present use rather than future use. It is not, generally, the loss of the proceeds of realization. This argument reinforces my view that in determining value to the owner, we cannot look merely to exit values.

Most of these comments have been addressed to the determination of value, not income. This is because it is value, not income, that is primary. The real investor problem, and the managerial problem, is to maximize present value: and income is the growth in present value which is achieved in the process of maximization. As Henry Simons pointed out long ago, income is merely a mathematical construction.[5] By seeking perfection in its measurement, we forego the opportunity to make presently attainable advances. For my part, I am prepared to settle for something less than perfection, to get material improvements which are already within our grasp.

---

[5] "Personal income may be defined as the algebraic sum of (1) the market value of rights exercised in consumption and (2) the change in the value of the store of property rights between the beginning and end of the period in question . . . . As Schäffle has said so pointedly, 'Das Einkommen hat nur buchhalterische Existenz.' It is indeed merely an arithmetic answer and exists only as the end result of appropriate calculations." Henry C. Simons, *Personal Income Taxation* (Chicago: University of Chicago Press, 1938, pp. 50–51).

# 6

## Current Issues about Current Costs

### by WILLIAM J. VATTER
#### UNIVERSITY OF CALIFORNIA, BERKELEY

ACCOUNTING reports and their content have been under increasing pressure for improvement in recent years. Accountants have been criticized for employing wide variations in method, and they have been accused of weakening their professional status by allowing choices between alternative procedures, which produce divergent results from similar data and which do not reflect properly the real results of business operations. In attempting to obtain solutions to these problems, some accountants take widely different positions as to the validity or the usefulness of different kinds of financial data, how that data should be reported, and what the results should be taken to mean.

Even when one finds a small group who have apparently similar aims and interests, the differences of opinion and method merely appear at another level. There are accountants who agree on the superiority of historical cost data but who disagree on the assignment of inventory costs and depreciation charges; they espouse discernibly different procedures to establish the production costs of specific lots of goods, and some of them will insist that period costs (those which do not respond to changes in the volume of operation) should be treated in a different manner from what they call product costs (those which do respond to changes in volume). Still other accountants will aver that historical cost data as a class are not adequate and that financial data, particularly costs, should be stated at current levels. Then, they differ about what *is* current cost, whether the adjustment

114

should be supplementary to the tracing of historical cost, or whether historical cost records are, in fact, relevant only for internal edification, and about whether historical cost should be transformed, ignored or discarded. Thus, it appears that if something should be done to bring current costs into the reporting pattern, there is question as to which current costs should be used, and how they should be handled. Some accountants insist that cost in financial reports should mean the current cost of replacement, which can be discovered by *ex post* application of current input prices to past production or other events. Others insist that reports should reflect extant opportunities in the market, and that exit prices (called net realizable value, current cash equivalent, or market opportunity cost) must be the final arbiters of asset value and the supposedly inseparable measurement of income.

Still another view is that values are inherently future-oriented, and, therefore, they ought to be stated to reflect the present value of expected future cash flows—even if we must use surrogates to quantify such data. But this approach is rejected by those who insist that one cannot measure future phenomena; this argument may take the form that measurement is not possible when the subject does not actually exist, but it is also expressed in terms of the requirement that reports should cover what *did* happen—not what may, or will happen. Both these objections may be couched in terms of objectivity as an essential of measurement, surrogates notwithstanding. But, at this point may be heard the voice of historical cost advocates, who insist on *their* kind of objectivity which is based on arms' length bargaining and legal rights and interpretations, and is supported by documentary evidence of transactions that did indeed occur!

There are still other side issues which color various positions; these evoke positions such as, that net realizable value cannot be relevant to the firm if it is really expected that the asset will be used; and that the present value of future services must be somewhat less than net realizable value, if the intention is to sell, and so on. The result of all this is a wide variety of choices and positions which cannot have any effect but confusion on the part of those who use accounting reports. And the stronger and more vigorous the argument about the choice among these viewpoints, the greater the confusion.

Now all of these positions cannot be wrong; for these ideas are advanced by serious and intelligent men, after much experience and careful consideration. In practice, one might be willing to consider that opinions could be swayed in one direction or another by the importunities of specific situations, such as the attempt to save a weak company and protect its shareholders from greater loss than might otherwise occur. Or, there may be a desire to promote a really sound entrepreneurial expansion by making the best of existing conditions and results. But, such considerations do not fit into the mold of theory, for theory in any field is that orderly and consistent structure of ideas—a basic frame of reference—which serves to systematize analysis, to standardize concepts and methods, to establish the continuity and validity of knowledge, to optimize understanding, and to maximize communication and the reliability of forecasts. Theory is not hypothesis, but synthesis; it must have continuity and realism; it must be operationally feasible; a theory which has no application or use does not deserve the name.

Scientific theories stand or fall on the test applied by continuous application—indeed, a forecast based on theory must fit facts, else either the application or the structure of theory is considered deficient. Accounting, being something less than a science, has not progressed very far in the empirical verification of theory, but the road is open, and some travelers have ventured on it a little way. That, however, is another issue.

The absence of verifiable forecasting does not alter the fact that accounting theory cannot really support different views of the same thing—the choice of method ought not to make different things look alike, or the same things look different. There stands a formidable problem which we here ignore—what are the criteria for different methods and what do those differences require (not what they may excuse) by way of method? All the papers presented here proceed from the assumption that the right method will produce the right result under the full range of conditions. Whether or not this assumption holds over the wide range of financial activities and conditions is a matter we presumably need not discuss. But I digress.

It has already been said that all the positions here reviewed cannot possibly be wrong; indeed, it would be expected by anyone who knows the people and their work, that *none* of them should be *entirely* wrong. These are not new positions, but for the most part, they have been held for some time and expressed through various media on different occasions. The persistence of these ideas is good reason for admiration—if not of the ideas themselves, then the courage and conviction of those who hold them.

It may be possible to understand this situation a little better if one examines those stated positions for similarities and differences. An attempt to do this leads one into some uncertain areas, for what one writes does not always reflect his entire thought processes. To extrapolate from the written word may be a bit dangerous, but necessary. Hopefully, it may precipitate better delineation of the general problem.

## I. Underlying Records

One item of some importance is the generally blithe assumption that whatever may be needed in the recording and analytical process will somehow be provided. Only one of those papers explicitly recognizes this issue in pointing out that

> Historical cost valuation is the only valuation method which includes, as an integral part of its valuation procedure structured on the double-entry bookkeeping system, the essential requirement of equity accounting that every actual change in the resources of an entity be recorded by relating inputs and outputs so that it can be traced and identified whenever necessary. (Ijiri, p. 13)

While this paper also points out that accounts *could* be kept in physical units, with appropriate valuation adjustments for reporting purposes, the author (Ijiri) is clearly concerned with the basic need to collect data under conditions that insure the recognition of events and changes. The rejection of changes in external prices is for him less important than is the assurance of an operationally complete record.

The omission of this in the other papers may be a tacit assumption that the historical cost record is superfluous. However, Professor Bell is quite willing to use historical cost data so long as they are supplemented by current cost information. He writes:

> . . . the use of current costs in accounting records in order to achieve the above advantages does not have to obviate employment of historic costs; indeed, the methods we employ build upon traditional accounting principles and keep track of historic costs both in daily internal records and in finished balance sheets and income statements. (Bell, p. 20)

But, Bell is also willing to throw away some of the recorded cost data at the end of the reporting period, replacing them with current entry costs; Staubus would make similar restatements but would use surrogates for discounted cash flows; but Chambers would settle for nothing but current exit prices or close approximations thereto. Only Bell seems to be really concerned that holding gains be separated and disclosed, even though he is not much concerned with intra-periodic fluctuations, so long as the beginning and closing position is adjusted.

## II. The Time-Continuum

These writers differ, as has already been noted, about the metaphysics of past versus future phenomena. Chambers insists that measurement cannot be applied to things or conditions which do not actually and currently exist. Staubus, however, maintains that

> . . . the external investor relies upon financial statements to help him predict aspects of the firm's future activities, e.g., earnings and dividends; the property of assets that he needs to know must have some relation to what will happen to the asset; the asset's past itinerary or a future course it could—but will not—take are activities that are not directly relevant to the investor's decision. (Staubus, p. 44)

Bell, in arguing for current cost in terms of entry value, writes:

> Accounting must measure past events, and to be useful, it must measure those which actually happened, not those which might happen if a firm does something other than that which was planned. (Bell, p. 30)

But, he seems not entirely satisfied with this; in the very next sentence he broadens his view to include some future data:

> As we have said, measure what has actually happened, then compare with what might happen now or in the future. (Bell, p. 30)

But, it is Ijiri who gives attention to the way in which the future may be predicted. He says:

> Historical cost valuation provides data that are useful for decisionmaking by insightful managers and investors insofar as history is the only basis for predicting the future. (Ijiri, p. 14)

He does not actually say that we can know or understand the future *only* in terms of an intelligent analysis of the past, but one gets the impression that he would not reject such a position. This idea—which one might expect to be at least accepted in principle by those who write about measurement—is either tacitly assumed or avoided in those papers.

### III. The Uses and Scope of Data

These papers differ also in their relative breadth of view concerning the scope of data to be recognized, and the way in which such information may be employed. For Chambers, there is no substitute nor any supplement to be derived from accounting data, for "current cash equivalent"—specific exit prices. At the other extreme, Staubus appears willing to accept (as the occasion may demand) various surrogates for his idealistic forecasted cash flows. His surrogates are clearly intended as compromises with practical issues in the real world. Ijiri seems to be the most concerned with practical considerations, when he writes:

> Historical cost valuation, by refusing to recognize holding gains and losses, is in line with the spirit of maintaining the status quo unless changes (in income) are proved to be necessary beyond any reasonable doubt. This spirit is essential for solving conflicts of interest and maintaining order and stability in society. (Ijiri, p. 13)

Both of these are quite different from the position taken by Bell, who adopts an attitude that would place the whole range of expectations, performance and revised plans in the province of the accountant; for he says:

> . . . the first task of any enterprise is to measure the profitability or performance of plans and decisions *which were actually made for some period ahead*, and thus evaluate performance against the expectations one originally had. (p. 27) . . . *then* the accountant, in conjunction with cost engineers, business planners, or what not, can go ahead and help to assess how to modify the existing or present plan of operation, or support the firm in adopting a new one. (Bell, p. 29)

Bell's view is colored by his economic model of the firm, not only in those statements, but in his rejection of Chambers' exit prices, which Bell finds incompatible with his concept of the firm:

> In these terms, Professor Chambers' concept of profit, if we understand it correctly, would have to be that a business plan would always have to be one of maximizing the acquirable cash equivalent of assets over successive short-run periods. This would seem to be where using the exit value or opportunity cost value of assets, period-by-period, to compare with current revenues leads us. For a firm dealing with anything more than the simplest retail or wholesale trading operations . . . such a view of the enterprise, its objectives, and its mode of thought, would just not seem to be applicable. (Bell, p. 28)

Some recognition of the constraints of the real world appears in Bell's discussion of exit prices as "opportunity costs." He observes, somewhat generously that, "Under certain ideal conditions, there may exist no difference in the two measures of current cost . . ." (p. 29). But he goes on to point out in great detail, the major requisites for the ideal market situation:

1. There must exist a large number of identical assets traded on one market so that market prices are known for both new and used assets;

2. The firm must have nondiscriminatory access to both the buying and selling sides of that market;

3. There must be no transportation or installation costs involved in either the purchase or the sale of the particular asset in question.[1]

Now, such conditions rarely, if ever, exist in the real world, so we are talking about two different concepts of current cost here. (Bell, p. 29)

A somewhat different aspect of pragmatism appears in Staubus' analysis. Perhaps because he starts with a completely future oriented view, he finds difficulty in quantifying the items in his system and he turns to realistic expedients for his answers. His closing illustration encompasses—for various assets—not only discounted cash flow, but also undiscounted cash flow, net realizable value, currently quoted market replacement cost, and a specific price index, to present what he calls the practical import of his argument.

Chambers does not emphasize practicality, but one gathers that it is the commonality of market price which for him expresses the relation of various kinds of accounting data to each other, and provides a direct medium for communicating accounting information. Indeed, it would appear that if assets do not have a quoted market price, or unless some equivalent value may be adduced, they are not reportable. This position is as practical as one can be with regard to the complexities of accounting analysis.

## IV. *Particulars of Application*

It is of some interest, that in this group of papers, we are not taken very far into the realm of specifics. Nobody seems concerned with

---

[1] Evidently Bell was thinking only of some specific kinds of assets. The list of specifications ought to include other conditions; at least, that the timing and quantities of purchase have no effect upon prices, and that all potential substitutes for materials, processes, or services are known and available to any interested firm.

how the current cost notion is to apply to those assets which by their nature do not have real counterparts in current market values. How does one establish the current cost of using a patent, copyright, franchise or leasehold? There is no real market price for highly specialized items such as these, neither is there a meaningful replacement cost, or specific price index. The cost of currently using such assets still involves computed amortization, unless one is willing to substitute the decline in market value. However, under inflationary conditions, the net change in market price may be an increase, a negative "cost." Is this acceptable? Or should we merely expense such an item immediately, when strictly relevant market values are not at hand? What is the market value of a tract of land that has been used for twenty years for industrial purposes, when a proposal is under consideration to convert the site to a parking lot for employees as soon as the new plant across the street is completed?

If a five-year-old lease of machinery is "really" a rental contract, should the expense element be computed as the annual net cash rent plus incidental costs, or should these be adjusted to agree with the market value of the property, or some specific index of lease rentals? If the contract is "really" a purchase, does the financing arrangement have anything to do with the cost? Should we be content to revalue the leased property annually to record expense, or should we employ a variable amortization applied to the capitalized market value, but also recognizing the terms of the lease? Yet if, as has been suggested in some quarters, the value of a lease contract should be established by discounting the future payments, which market rate should be used—the rate implied by a comparison of market price of the asset with the contractual cash flow, the current cost of capital to the lessor, or some other presumably equivalent market rate offered by some selected financing institutions?

This brings to the fore another question which deserves attention. It will be observed that none of the papers presented here has paid any attention to the current-value issues related to debt and equity. If we are to record accounts receivable at discounted amounts, shouldn't we use the same approach to the presentation of debt? And if we use current prices for securities owned (which are, inherently, reflections of the market rate of return), shouldn't we use current prices for securities issued? Recently we have seen corporate borrowing rates move rapidly higher; first grade utility bonds have been priced to yield around 9–10 percent. If we use market rates to evaluate corporate debt, we could get some interesting results. Suppose a company has outstanding $155 million, 5 percent debt running for 18 years, with unamortized discount of $13 million. At a market rate of 8 percent, the present worth of the future cash payments on these debts works out to $111,038,244. This reduction of debt amounts to $31 million, net. Is this income, realized or realizable gain, or capital adjustment?

On the other hand, there are changes in market price of the outstanding stock—the obligation to shareholders. During this same period, the market price of the company's common shares fell from $130 to $39. Applied to 14,250,000 shares, this decline amounts to 1 *billion* 300 million dollars. Data to convert this company's assets to market values are not at hand; but the total assets in the conventional statement are 1 billion 699 million, and the common stock equity appears as $621 million. How much is left after adjustment? The company has not been engaged in any new operations, and its products are not discredited; the most recent report of this company showed earnings of $3.60 per share, up 22 percent from the previous year. The reported income would hardly be reduced much by substituting current costs, for the prices of most of the kinds of assets the company uses changed but little in the past year. Situations like this suggest that there are some hard questions here to which we have given little attention.

## V. *Single Measure Emphasis*

Much divergence of thought in accounting arises from the effort to establish the one perfect measure of whatever it is that accountants attempt to deal with. But, accounting is certainly concerned with something more than the asset values that appear in balance sheets. It is, therefore, a bit disconcerting that two of the papers concern themselves almost exclusively with how we should state assets, presumably because the change in residual equity thus determined *is* income. The difference between those papers, however, is much greater than this would suggest—the wide variety of asset measurements which Staubus would employ as surrogates for the cash-flow essence of value is not at all compatible with the Chambers position.

But is it really true that the work of accounting is important only at that instant when one year closes so that another may begin?

Looking past the specific words and phrases of these papers, it is hard to imagine why we would put together a balance sheet or any other report—however the amounts were established—unless there was something to be gained from the effort. But what *is* to be gained from accounting reports? Is it some one amount—net income after taxes, total assets, earnings retained for the period, the maximum legal dividend limit? Is it a single ratio—fully diluted net earnings per share, rate of return on investment or percentage income to sales? Or is it more likely to be an analysis of financial events, in terms that give the reader an array of data that may help him to understand why the income is what it is, and how the position got that way?

## VI. *Data for Decision Makers*

The inescapable generality of accounting data is an important factor here. The accountant cannot really meet the needs of some unknown reader, even if we characterize him with the label of investor or stockholder. For one thing, the information needs of individual investors or stockholders are as different as their objectives are different. If the objective is growth with minor regard for risk, the investor's needs are not the same as when his objective is stability, safety of principal and a steady dividend flow. If he seeks diversification, there must be some way to trace it; the relative productivity and progress of foreign operations, time horizons in expansion, the degree of effort in research and development, are important, especially when expressed in financial terms. Comparisons in the marketplace are not the whole story; we need to analyze and compare results and conditions within the firm in meaningful terms.

In this connection, I was delighted to see Bell take the position that a comparison of achievements as reported, with plans actually made for that period, is a basic need; that it is the accountants' task to provide data for that evaluation. He goes on to say, "Once this is done, *then* one can compare the cost of continuing to use the assets . . . as opposed to acquiring and using some other assets . . ." (p. 28). This should focus our attention upon the basic issue of corporate reporting.

Those who manage enterprises financed with other people's money have a responsibility beyond merely reporting what they have done, or allowing accountants to do this. I have wondered for a long time why managers are not willing—even anxious—to present at one annual meeting a special kind of accounting statement, similar to that presented to key officers and the board of directors, which would set forth the program for the next period in summary budget form. Not only would this serve to indicate in concrete terms the general pattern of activities and expectations, but it would also serve as a basis for interpreting the results of operations as reported at the end of the period. Internal management is programmed in this way, because there is no better way to evaluate managers than to compare the considered, feasible, and desirable plan with what is actually found to be accomplished—of course, making allowance for identifiable changes. If this tool serves when officers and directors evaluate their own work, it ought to be useful when shareholders evaluate their investment. And perhaps Ijiri's suggestions of commitment accounting and shorter reporting intervals ought to be taken seriously. The problems of reporting results over a short period are not really so formidable if we do not insist on the determination of income and full details of financial position. The current transactions of sales, costs and fund flows can report much concerning operating conditions and efficiency.

The great bulk of all accounting is and should be concerned with such matters, for the maintenance of efficient operations, the current adjustments needed to align with changed conditions, and other similar data are not merely the private concern of those who operate within the corporate shield. One of the prices for public financing and corporate autonomy should be disclosure—not grudging admission concealed in accountants' footnotes, but in clear presentations which indicate what goes on and why. This may have to be done (as it often is within the firm) in such a way as to separate operating efficiency from the effects of price changes.

Again, quite apart from the effects of *changes* in price, there are relationships *within* the structure of prices (as they exist at a given time) which have much to do with the amount of income that will eventually be reported. These relationships and the resultant alternatives in trading margins are not entirely controllable by management, though the forces of sales promotion and advertising obviously attempt to produce greater volume of sales and to offset the impact of prices by suggestions about quality, service, prestige, and other features of the firm's products. But, in this area and within any given price structure, managerial choices may affect the allocation of resources and the production of income through decisions about which markets are to be entered, to what degree, and through what approaches. This is part of the reason behind the pressure for disclosure of events by major lines of activity which has gained attention in recent years.

## VII. Facets of Price Change

Moving from the kinds of reporting information mentioned up to this point, we approach the general issue of price changes. In general, there are three areas in which variations in price have substantial effect; the first is inventory; the second is long-term assets; the third—not given a great deal of specific attention in the papers presented here—is investments in other companies. Perhaps the lack of emphasis on investments is because the practice generally is followed to disclose the market values of investment securities, when those holdings are not locked in by affiliations or similar constraints. Perhaps the recent experience with securities prices—and their response to psychological rather than economic factors—has had some restraining influence.

However, it seems fundamental to me that adjustments to reflect current costs ought to recognize the effect of price changes as separate influences in the profit picture. This should be done because of the intrinsically different nature of transaction or trading profits and holding or price-profits. Not only should these two different elements be reported separately, but the computations should be more than a mere year-end adjustment. To state beginning and ending inventories on a current price basis and use only these figures to adjust the flow of costs through inventory buries part of the price profit in the cost of goods sold, in much the same way as LIFO procedures bury price-profit in inventory balances, while FIFO procedures bury it in the gross margin figure. If we really want to see the effect of price changes, we must have a way to compare current costs and past costs; the operations within the year need analysis so far as inventories are concerned.

There is a technique for this—standard cost and variance analysis with respect to price changes. The information that could be reported by using this approach—even in summary terms—could be much more revealing than that to be had from mere re-pricing of annual inventory carryovers. Price data of this kind are especially valuable when, as is often the case, some price changes are involuntary and uncontrollable, and others may be optional or planned speculations. Unless such analysis is made, managers may be credited with achievements which really arise from luck or outside influences, quite beyond their control.

Another set of price effects may be buried in revenue figures. Different lines of product may exhibit quite different mixes of volume and price-change effects. Such data could be analyzed and reported in at least summary terms. A strong concern for showing the effects of changing prices would suggest that data of this kind would provide a realistic basis for the analysis that would promote understanding and provide a better basis for evaluating future prospects.

With respect to long term assets, the problem of adjusting costs to more current levels is both more difficult and of less current interest to the investor. Markets for specialized assets of the plant and equipment category are less perfect than those for materials and supplies. While there are organized markets for some assets in this class, highly individualized items are likely to be restated only in terms of appraisals, in which the use of specific or more general price indexes is hardly escapable, if only because of the complexity of the task.

But, there is also the problem exemplified by assets held for standby use, or operations of secondary importance. While these often are worth less in the market than it would cost to dispose of them, they may still be able to produce at a low enough marginal cost to warrant their retention for less precise operations, for lower quality product, or to fill in during peak loads. Their value may be only the amount they may save if the need for their services happens to arise.

However, long term assets raise another problem of measurement, apart from the gross figure at which they are stated; there is an issue of how much it costs to use them for a period. However much we may wish it were otherwise, some measure of depreciation must be provided. Professor Chambers is quite willing to let successive market prices determine this, not without some degree of justification, for at some time, the asset will be disposed of and whatever has been the carrying amount will disappear. However, the year by year use of market quotations may or may not provide a measure of the user cost which depreciation ought to represent. If the services of an asset were unaffected by any use to which it might be put, if maintenance and repair were systematically to be depended on, and if knowledge about such assets and their potential employments were public information, there might be more confidence in market prices as measures of asset values in this category. But even so, many things can happen to distort the relationship between the decline of asset value and the user cost. The reason I continue to operate my car has nothing whatever to do with the price of cars labeled with the same name and of the same vintage; rather, it is because my private knowledge of the services to be had from that car is better than that of the car-buying public. I know the maintenance record of this car, and I know much more of its operating and want-satisfying characteristics than anyone else will either know or believe.

There is one more important consideration with regard to long term assets—the responsibility for the various decisions that are made about them. There is the decision to acquire them in the first place; the rightness or wrongness of that decision ought to be evaluated separately from the decision to continue it in service during this year. But, the acquisition is reflected in the carrying *amount* as well as the remaining service-potentials; the holding gain, if any, ought to be separated from the current usage of the asset. A purely market based depreciation charge shows only the current value-decline, which may come about by purely technical and temporary price situations. One can see good reason for Bell's separation of current year depreciation adjustments from what he calls "realiz*able* cost savings"; the difference is not merely a matter of syntax. Realizable cost savings are the current interpretation of those *future* depreciation adjustments which we hope *will* be "earned." Thus, they are adjustments of invested capital rather than income of any kind. So long as the firm is "locked in" by the nature of its business commitments to a continued use of specified assets, the future depreciation adjustments for such assets represent merely the additional investment that currently higher prices force the first to maintain.

Quite another kind of holding gain arises from assets not subject to the "lock-in" referred to. In the case of marketable investments, the option to sell is unrestricted; the gain is, in fact, realizable. While it may be an open question as to whether such a gain represents *earned* income (Bell's phrase), it is income, even though its special nature would suggest that it be reported separately.

Last among the long-term price effects is the matter of general price-level adjustments. Ijiri gives this issue scant attention—perhaps because the way his subject is defined precluded its discussion. The Chambers position appears to limit general price level adjustments to an analysis of cash balances, so as to show in residual equity the loss from holding dollars in a rising price level (or vice versa). All of the recognized assets and liabilities in the Chambers model would already be stated in current dollars *qua* exit prices. Thus, the effects of *changing* prices of other assets or liabilities would be buried with other details in the one-number effect of repricing asset or debt items.

Staubus is but little enchanted with price level adjustments, except as a possible last resort when no other surrogate is available. Bell is the only writer in this group who gives general price level adjustments a place in his analysis—and then, only as secondary to specific price changes. Presumably this is because the two factors of price change may sometimes move in different degrees and directions during certain time intervals.

Now it may be true, as Bell quotes Mathews, that

> Data which are measured in different units to begin with cannot be converted to a common basis of measurement merely by applying a common conversion factor . . . (Bell, p. 25)

but, one may also note that all prices are ratios of value between some commodity and all other commodities as expressed in the monetary unit at a given moment. One certainly cannot compare the dollars used to acquire a bond investment with those in which it is settled at maturity, unless one assumes that the two kinds of dollars actually can be used in a comparable market. Thus, it would appear open to question whether the specific prices that make up the general price level are more or less important than the general level itself.

Of course, Bell does not really dispense with the general price level adjustment; he recognizes its usefulness for interfirm and interperiod comparisons, for he writes,

> The fact of the matter is that comparisons among firms at a moment of time, and of trends in one firm over time serve as the primary valid reason for adjusting *properly constructed* income and balance sheet data for changes in the value of the dollar. (Bell, p. 26)

The inserted italics serve to call attention to Bell's reluctance to accept any part of the idea that a general price level adjustment lessens the need for reflecting current entry prices; but this emphasis seems to imply also that adjustments to reflect entry prices should precede the general price level adjustment, if that is made. However, it would seem possible to make a case for the position that, in comparing holding gains as between firms, the general price level adjustment could precede the reflection of specific prices. The requirement that general price level adjustments should be applied only to properly constructed statements is less acceptable when one cannot find (in these four papers, at least) any substantial consensus of what "properly constructed" means.

It should not be necessary to wait until all these various preferences and doubts are resolved before there is any recognition of changing prices in financial reports. While accountants argue proprieties or arrange compromises (if indeed they can), it is still essential to maintain communication with those who read financial reports. Whether or not we—or anyone else—may like it, markets and prices being what they are and indexes being what *they* are, the readers of financial reports will receive the accountants' message only in terms of *their* receptual referents. They see dollars as they see them; and to them, a dollar is a dollar.

In closing, it may be well to review the area of discussion in a somewhat different vein. It has already been suggested that no one set or combination of ideas from the four papers is conclusively satisfying. All of the authors are concerned with the same bundle of problems, but each sees them in a different light, and there is very little consensus in what remains after an attempt at comparison and analysis. As stated earlier, none of these positions is really wrong, nor is any of them really right, for the problem is not so simple as to be solved by a single formula or a stereotyped procedure. What is needed is an open-minded attempt to put together all those techniques that may produce useful results.

There has been considerable reference in these papers to the notion of relevance, and with good reason; decision-making must be based on relevant information. But, relevance is not an inherent characteristic of data, nor a way of viewing markets or measurement methods. Relevance is the degree to which data reflect the relations that exist (or ought to exist) between problems and their resolution in the decision process. If we were certain of the precise nature of all the problems and goals of our readers, we could do a better job of adapting our methods to fit *their* needs. However, there are two impediments to this. One is that the responsibility for financial reports and what they may present is not exclusively delegated to accountants. The other is that given the wide variety of uses to which accounting data may be put, it is quite possible for the accountant to actually hinder the decision process, rather than assist it, by putting too much emphasis on his condensation of data to make it fit some neat reporting format. One pervasive risk which accompanies every effort to summarize, simplify, or sharpen the impact of messages is that potentially valuable data may be overlooked, "swamped out," or thrown away through the very zeal which motivates the data processor. Worse, the attempt to select the relevant data at the pre-message level can preempt the decision process itself. An assumption about what the problem or decision to be made is and may involve leads us easily to a further assumption about what the decision maker *ought* to want. This may look like relevance, but it cannot be; relevance implies full knowledge of goals, situations, value systems and abilities of the decision-maker. Only the user of financial data can know (and even then imperfectly) what is, in fact, relevant to the problem with which he is confronted.

Accountants are observers, analysts, and interpreters as well as reporters. The first three tasks are prerequisites for intelligent discharge of the other one. We ought to try to find ways of reporting all the pertinent and reliable data which can be honestly used to evaluate the operations that are the subject of our reports. This includes many things besides price changes and their effects.

# 7

## Appraising the Four Schools

### *by* DONALD J. BEVIS
TOUCHE, ROSS & CO.

THIS symposium reminds me of an Accounting Principles Board
meeting. We cannot agree here; in many of our Board meetings
we also have difficulty in finding agreement. I would like to suggest
to those of you who criticize the Board that you reflect on the difficulty
of finding agreement here prior to issuing further criticism.

I have read the papers, I have listened to the summarizations, I
have heard the discussions, and the principal conclusion that I draw
from all of this is that something must be done. I have not been convinced by any of the speakers as to how assets and income should be
measured or presented. But I am convinced that something must be
done.

I think fair value accounting is a necessity. It should be mandatory
with, of course, the appropriate disclosure. This to me is "economic
realism." Everyone, including the historical cost accounting school,
is arguing for a change. If we are to serve the investor, especially
considering the effects of inflation, technological changes, changes in
social philosophies, and changes in consumer desires, I do not think
we can ignore this need for change. Further, I think management
needs something better to aid it in decision-making in order to appraise their alternative courses of action. I agree with George Catlett's
comment that the problem is determining what best presents the facts
to users of financial statements.

I also agree with Yuji Ijiri that we cannot abandon the historical
cost accounting concept. But, in my opinion, fair value accounting

131

can and should be integrated into our basic financial statements. This is a disclosure problem, and I think that is where part of our problem lies. We should be able to measure holding gains and losses and then disclose them. The investor should be able to appraise management decisions and its alternative courses of action.

That historical cost accounting is the least costly, as has been argued, is, in my opinion, quite debatable. Even if it is least costly, you must pay for progress, and progress will not be made by maintaining the status quo. As a matter of fact, it is just as expensive to furnish the supplementary information that Ijiri would permit as it would be to integrate it into the basic financial statements. It seems to me that historical cost accounting fails its objective when cost is no longer a valid measure of whatever we are dealing with. Historical cost accounting can be the least useful measure and therefore, when compared to its benefits, it can be the most expensive. We all know that historical cost accounting does not always determine what can be paid out in dividends, as in a period of inflation, for example.

Though the problem of objectivity disturbs me, I do not believe it should be a deterrent to change. We all know that historical cost accounting is debatable and subject to disputes; witness our many problems today in dealing with our old conventions. Therefore, I would again repeat that objectivity should not disturb us if we can find a more useful measure.

We rely too much, I believe, on our convention of realization. I would like to redefine that convention. I believe that I could support the contention, both logically and in an economic sense, that realization is accrual. Some of you, I know, will disagree with me. But if we could accept that, we could get rid of such terms as "operating income," "realized income," "earned income," etc., and we could concentrate on measuring one concept, namely, income.

Price level accounting which is based on historical cost accounting is in many cases a better measure of income than is traditional historical cost accounting. But, it also has its deficiencies. It does not recognize technological changes. It does not permit evaluation of alternative courses of action.

I am not arguing for entry replacement costs, exit opportunity costs, current costs, or current resale prices. What I am arguing for is fair value accounting. When I speak of fair value accounting, I include in the definition the use of present values, if appropriate, or other measurement devices if they are more appropriate. I believe fair value accounting is most responsive to the going concern concept, which I accept and which one speaker here has rather casually dismissed. Professor Amey pointed out that there must be an intent of holding and/or using—that we are not dealing with liquidation. I agree and therefore, I think it is quite important that we reaffirm the going concern concept. My definition of fair value accounting also contemplates recognition of technological changes, other uses of assets, market demand, time and place utility, etc. Paul Rosenfield pointed out at least one defect of replacement cost accounting. Despite this defect, replacement cost does meet the test of fair value in some instances.

George Staubus bases his argument on relevance. I would substitute usefulness as a more appropriate criterion. His answers, I believe, in the main would be the same. Ray Chambers, however, points out that usefulness is seldom defined and attempts to substitute "functional" which is of no help, being equally ill-defined. Actually, this is our first problem requiring resolution. I think with adequate research we could develop a useful definition of "usefulness." It is a people definition. We cannot develop concepts unless we know what users need and what is useful to them. I also would add that Ray does use the word "useful" in his own exposition; therefore, he must have felt that it had some significant meaning. The other three authors also use the word "useful." I have also noted that all the commentators around the table have used the word "useful" at least once. So, I would therefore again repeat, let us define "usefulness."

Frank Weston has pointed out the weaknesses in Chambers' approach, and I will only state here that I generally agree with Weston's comments. If Chambers' philosophy prevails in Australia, I am going to move there and, through take-over bids, take over all of Australia on an under valued basis.

I compliment the paper-preparers and propose that we borrow from all of them in the resolution of our problem. An immediate solution is demanded, one that is understandable to informed users and will become a fundamental of generally accepted accounting principles. I am not enamored, however, of that term, "generally accepted accounting principles." The application of fair value accounting should be continuous. It cannot be desultory; it requires continuous review to be effective and to be useful.

In conclusion, I would like to suggest that our staying power for argumentation should now be applied to develop appropriate measurement and presentation techniques. We have found that the development of measurement and presentation techniques, at least in the APB, brings forth other problems. Therefore, I support Oscar Gellein in suggesting that we prepare detailed financial statements under each of the proposed methods. They will disclose other problems that none of us have as yet visualized.

# 8

## The Income Concept Complex: Expansion or Decline

### by NORTON M. BEDFORD
UNIVERSITY OF ILLINOIS

IN the debate on the impact of reason versus the impact of emotion upon the actions of man, one is hard pressed whichever position one elects to defend. It seems that in the endeavor to communicate and gain acceptance, any dinner-speaker message sender ought, from time to time, to shift his medium from reason to the "poetic." This explains the fable of King Income, which will now be related. The facts presented are not proven. Rather, the effort is merely to present a picture that will not be soon forgotten, with the supposition that once the picture is viewed, one thousand reasoning men will provide one thousand reasons to support that view.

The story is about a mighty king who lives in a land of Might Have Been. Strongest of the strong and wisest of the wise was he, and all his loyal subjects followed him faithfully and believed him to be the best possible directing force for all activities throughout the land. Under this king with such loyal supporters, this land of Might Have Been grew and grew in affluence and in power.

Then one dark, wintery day, one loyal subject of this mighty King Income, for that was indeed his name, was heard to say in a rather melancholy way, "I think the king needs counsel in the running of this great land. He ought to listen to Prince LIFO." No sooner had he spoken than up rose a learned professor who straightway shot him dead and proclaimed loud and clear, that not Prince LIFO but Prince FIFO was, by far, the better advisor for King Income.

Now, when the king learned of this little incident, he was exceedingly disturbed. "I must not have this unrest in the land," thought he. So for 40 days and 40 nights this wisest of mortal kings sat in his thinking chamber wearing his best reasoning cap. He then emerged and issued a mighty proclamation that divided the kingdom into six overlapping princedoms, under Prince FIFO, Prince LIFO, Prince Money Value, Prince Real Value, Prince All-inclusive, and Prince Dirty Surplus. Because the six princes were part of King Income's family, all the loyal subjects, who could choose to live in whichever princedom they wished, recognized that there had been no real change: they were merely governed by the Income family instead of the figurehead of that family. Oh, there was a Professor Hicks, who said something about the breaking apart of the land, but no one paid much attention to him because he was well known as a theorist, anyway. So, on this basis of princedoms, the kingdom of the Income family waxed strong and affluent for 1,000 years more.

But, then was born a descendant of that melancholy one who had been shot by that learned professor on that most fateful day. By name he was known as "Troublesome Joe," and he, too, met his fate on a bleak and bleary day in a most disturbing way, when he observed that none of the princedoms were able to satisfy his varying needs and that he would prefer to be governed by different, varying and then non-existent income governments. It was even rumored, after his demise, that Troublesome Joe had wanted to be governed by many different income governments at the same time.

Even though his advisors told him that Troublesome Joe was a "free thinker" and would not watch television longer than two hours a day, old King Income recognized a problem when he saw one, and he thought his rule might be near its end, for he had no more sons and could never hope to govern separately the almost infinite number of income governments called for by this "Troublesome" one. But, remember, he was the wisest of the wise, so he donned his best reasoning hat (his subjects had given him a hat to replace the reasoning cap he had worn out during the 40-day and 40-night session 1,000 years ago) and retired to his highest thinking chamber where for 100 days and 100 nights, he pondered. When he emerged, worn and haggard, he triumphantly proclaimed, "I am still king! But, we will have a premier, my cousin 'Operational Income,' who will create a vast complex government system which will provide various governing systems flexible enough to provide whatever guidance each subject could want in any conceivable time, place and situation." (The king had used the term "system" rather than "government" because one of his professors had told him that all modern thinking was in terms of systems.)

But before the new premier, Operational Income, could really develop his governing system, some of the scholars of the university started a student protest under the banner, "The king is dead. We want freedom from the Income family."

Now, all of this really disturbed the mighty king, and he directed a scholar, known as the "Bearded One," to call a conference in the area nearby the River Kaw to decide what should be done. This great conference is now in process, and throughout the land of Might Have Been, people sit glued to their television sets awaiting the decision that will solve the problems of their beloved king. Thus far, the discussion on methods of measuring income seems to have centered on the "image" of King Income which should be held out to all subjects of the land of Might Have Been. The question of overthrowing the kingdom seems beyond consideration, and those who opt for an expansion of the kingdom are somewhat guarded in their utterances. Only by an overall synthesis of the analyses of these Illustrious Ones is the call of the trumpet not uncertain in proposing an expansion of the income concept complex.

Now, having painted the abstract picture and communicated with the "poetic" ones, one must seek to reason with the reasoning ones. So, starting with a somewhat philosophical base, consider the possibility that there is a moral to the fable. It is that because all institutions of man change, only those professions that adjust their institutional underpinnings to the needs of society survive. The moral is based on the fact that there is a condition of continuous entropy throughout the world. Now, this condition requires a continuous adjustment or replacement of those concepts used to organize and direct human society and individual activity. Only by adjustment or replacement of concepts can man combat the enervating tendency toward disorder and restore that order conducive to better human life.

A corollary of this proposition is that the longer a concept exists in society and the more it is used, the more complex man tends to make it. History suggests that growing complexity is the nature of measured income, and the philosophy of entropy would suggest that this complexity arises as man seeks to overcome the inroads of natural disorder upon ordered life.

Turning now to the concept of income as a human construct and considering its nature, one cannot help but be aware that income is merely a stimulating force which causes a great deal of human activity. While one tends initially to think of the desire for income as the motivating force, the perception hereby submitted is that income, itself, is the stimulus that triggers action. It is the carrot pursued for whatever cause. Just as the well-fed fox pursues the rabbit, the instinct to pursue income is so ingrained in the human system that income alone is the stimulus for action. In fact, just as the mechanical rabbit replaces the live one in the dog race, any measured income can replace a basic income that might once have been.

Postponing for the moment (in the belief that realization will come with awareness) any further effort to provide evidence that there is no one, basic income concept having a universally determinable nature, it seems appropriate to examine the income concept as it is now measured by accountants. As one views the generally accepted alternative accounting principles, it must be obvious that measured income, as it now exists, is not a single valued amount. Periodic income measured using LIFO procedures is normally a different amount from income measured using FIFO or income measured using various replacement costs or various realizable cash amounts. Yet, for different purposes, each measure might have a use, in that each stimulates the appropriate action. Not only are different measured income amounts used for different purposes, but the existence of human and environmental instability factors suggest that any measurement is merely a probability. The point is that not only does it appear that no one, basic, precise income concept exists but also various measured amounts of income have different roles to play in different times, places, and situations. The conclusion is that the income concept is now no longer a single concept but a complex of concepts. As a complex, one must constantly be aware of the particular aspect of it under discussion at any point in time, place or situation. If this is not possible, it may indeed be time to substitute the notion of "information for decision-making" for the notion of "income." Should this occur, it would be appropriate to refer to the shift of interest from "income" to "information" as a decline in the relative role of the income complex in society. On the other hand, should it appear that the income concept has not yet become so complex that it needs to be abandoned, one should refer to further refinement of it both in preciseness of single measurement and in different measurements for different purposes as an expansion of the complex. Implicit in this notion of expansion or decline of the income concept is a rejection of the notion that greater or less use of some type of a standardized income measurement represents an expansion or decline of the income concept complex in society. In fact, the two notions of expansion and decline are antithetical, because a crystalization of interest on one concept would probably result in an expansion of the use of that concept, but such a development would represent a decline in the scope of the total income concept complex.

In order to examine the income concept and its future in society, it seems appropriate to recognize it as a human construct useful for motivating action. That is, it is not a discovered feature of mankind. At its best, it can be a means for explaining human action. At second best, it can be a broad surrogate for a multitude of physical and psychological features of man.

But, as a human construct useful for organizing society, it has been a most effective device for developing civilizations. Furthermore, the historical evidence, meager as it is, suggests that as it has been more precisely defined, it has contributed more to the development of civilizations. Witness the rise of South Germany in the 16th century as the income concept was articulated as a measured amount; the development of stable governments as the income concept was even more precisely defined for income tax purposes and other governmental uses; and the development of peoples capitalism as the income concept construct was applied to the public disclosure need of investors.

Of the two views of the income concept complex—as a human construct and as a discovered phenomenon of man—the former appears to be the more useful. In fact, the second view, that the desire for a universal basic income is the force motivating human activity, tends to fade away in relevance in an advanced society where the sensitive wants of man are those higher up the scale than the economic one in the hierarchy of human wants. Thus, when measured income is viewed as a reflection of the extent to which the discovered wants of a man are satisfied, it becomes apparent that in modern society we may indeed be in the twilight of the income concept.

But, as a human construct useful for coordinating social and economic life, the income concept complex may be most useful and should be expanded to meet the needs of modern society. However, such a house of income will be no better than its foundation. When one examines alternative foundations, one concludes that the expanded income concept complex needed for modern society will have to rest on a foundation of either "operationalism" or "value."

Despite the disenchantment of the psychologists with operationalism in the basic disciplines, the inability of accountants, specifically, and society in general to articulate a precise constitutive concept of income may leave operational measures as the only option available.

Operationalism holds that the concept is synonymous with the operations involved in measuring income. Thus, if several sets of operations were available to measure income, each set of measurement operations would represent a different concept of income. Unless the set of operations used in measuring income is specified, there is always the possibility of misunderstanding. In an ideal sense, operationalism also requires that the environment in which the measurement occurred be specified. Without a specification of the environment, doubt may arise as to the nature, validity and accuracy of the measurement. For example, a measure of depreciation would not be operationally complete until the degree of possible error in estimating the life of the resource was specified. If made by an optimistic person, one measurement determining factor might differ from that which would prevail if a pessimistic person made the estimate. Idealism, however, is probably never to be the lot of the income measurement, and it may be necessary to exclude a precise description of the environment from the operational measure. Nevertheless, it does not seem unrealistic to propose that there be drawn up several sets of income measurement operations and several sets of environmental reliability conditions, which could be specified in measuring income in any particular time, place, or situation. Thus, income measured according to operational set $A$ in Condition $I$ would provide an income measure having a more precise meaning than would any one uniformly measured income figure. Acceptance of the operational point of view would certainly acquaint society with the fact that there is more than one income concept and would lend a preciseness to the income measurement that does not now prevail under the many alternative accounting procedures available.

The basic objection to operational income is, that to measure, one must have something to measure. This holds that there must be a flow of merchandise before one can measure that flow. It follows that to measure income, there first must exist income; for measurement is merely the assignment of numbers to things. Actually, there are so many rules by which numbers may be assigned to a flow of merchandise that this notion of measurement is of limited use. If these rules for assigning numbers to things are specified in detail, the measurement process is pretty much an operational procedure. If alternative measurement rules are allowed, various sets of measurement rules would result in various number assignments to things. But, this is insufficient justification for the operational approach, for critics contend that there did exist a constitutive thing, the flow of merchandise, and that, though different measurement operations may exist, the resulting measurements in every case are dependent upon the existence of the thing—the flow of merchandise. In this context, income measurement is, in part, based on operationalism and, in part, on the existence of a constitutive thing. In terms of the dog race, the rabbit is real, but he is observed with many different sets of eyes.

But, one is inclined to raise the question of whether or not civilization in general, and accountants in particular, have now developed to the stage where it is appropriate to recognize and be guided by the proposition that things, as well as measurements, are operational in nature. They are merely the perceptions of man. In fact, most perceived things are merely perceived attributes or features of things that operationally can be changed.

The proposition is that people are rapidly moving to the level where the scorned philosophers' proposition that all that exists is perception may have to be accepted. This is a fundamental proposition. It assumes that mankind is about ready to jerk himself free from his historically conditioned responses. If this proposition does indeed become accepted, it will mean that man has assumed human responsibility for the development of civilization. No longer will man be able to fall back upon his tradition-taught insights as to the nature of the real world. His destiny will be in his own hands.

Let me hasten to say that mankind has evolved so much as a homogeneous animal that his perceptions are very much in common. This homogeneous aspect of all human nature is, thus, the basis for the assumption that a constitutive thing exists which can be measured.

But, as one examines developments in accounting disclosures, one is struck with the realization that accountants and society are constantly observing new things to measure. The recognition of leases as assets and liabilities is probably the most obvious thing accountants have recently decided to admit that they perceive. Pollution costs seem to be a new thing on the horizon. Of course, neither accountants nor society have devised criteria for deciding how to go about deciding what perceptions shall be recognized as things. When this is done, things as well as measurement will be based on operationalism rather than on the notion of a constitutive thing.

The point is that operationalism may not be an impossible base for the income concept complex which is rapidly developing in our society. The accounting interpretation of operationalism is, of course, still quite crude, but operationalism is now so much a part of accounting that it seems appropriate to recognize it.

The advantages of operationalism as the base for an expanded income measurement function in society are many. Operationalism is in accord with the philosophy of pragmatism which has made America great; it works. It provides a flexibility for accounting theory that is not now evident in the literature. But, its greatest contribution will be that readers of income reports will realize that the meaning, in a constitutive sense, of any measured income can be understood only by knowing how the income was measured, that is, the operations undertaken by the accountant to produce the measured income amount. In that sense, income measured using a set of operations including the LIFO procedure is a different concept of income than that derived by using another set which includes the FIFO but excludes the LIFO procedure. Similarly, income figures excluding or including "capital" gains would represent different concepts of income. The notion would prevail that different concepts of income exist and that no income measure should be used without determining the operational process by which and for which it was measured. If both multi-dimensional and multiple valued measurements are indeed the needs of modern society, as *A Statement of Basic Accounting Theory*[1] contends, an operational base for the expanded income concept complex would seem to afford the flexibility needed for that structure.

The only realistic alternative to operationalism as a base for the emerging income concept complex in society is a structure based on economic value. Under it, any measured amount of income would be good or bad depending upon the extent to which it corresponded to the increase or decrease in economic value. In the context that income is an increase in economic value, accounting research presumably would be directed to improving existing accounting measures of income to make them accord more with that standard than has prevailed in the past.

But, what is value? To begin with, it is necessary to distinguish the value of things from the values of people. It is the values of people which give value to things. That is, the tastes, attitudes, opinions, and beliefs of people cause them to want, in varying degrees of intensity, those things that will enable the person to realize his values. Presumably, a "thing" that has a capacity to enable people to realize many different values might have a greater market or exchange value than a "thing" with a smaller capacity for the realization of human values. Now, since price (exchange value) is normally less or equal to the capacity of a "thing" to enable a person to realize his values, one must conclude that as a measure of value, market price is not a realistic departure point for measuring income in terms of want satisfaction.

It is, presumably, want satisfaction or capacity to satisfy wants that represents the basic value base which should be used for developing an income measurement. And, this gets us back into the marshy part of the land of certain philosophical and sociological concepts. The implication is that the value planks for a foundation for the income concept complex are not as sturdy as they initially seemed. The apparent fact is that economists have always had a rather limited view of the notion of value.

It is important to remember that the value of a "thing" can be changed merely by changes in the minds of persons, as the psychological impact of the post-1929 depression so vividly destroyed balance

---

[1] *A Statement of Basic Accounting Theory* (Evanston, Illinois: American Accounting Association, 1966).

sheet asset values. In fact, if one recognizes that the instability of the beliefs and opinions of the human mind is much greater than the instability of the social and physical environment in which man lives, one might conclude that market value accounting may result in much greater fluctuations in income than would an accrual process, where the impact of the fluctuation of human opinion and beliefs were minimized to some degree. The assumption is that the human mind tends to exaggerate changes in the social and physical environment, and these exaggerations will cause greater fluctuations in market prices than would otherwise prevail.

The one thing that is clear from all analyses of the future of the income concept is that more precise measurements are going to be needed in the future. The present concept of income is a rather crude concept in the same way that a sledge hammer is a crude concept of the woodsman's ax. Income is crude, both in concept and in measurement. Yet, it is the most effective device so far constructed by man to organize society. The only possible substitute on the horizon is the even cruder concept of "information." Thus, by default, it seems that the role of the income concept will have to increase in the future. This suggests that accountants should improve their measured income amounts to accommodate the developing society. Realistically, they ought to adopt the operational concept to facilitate the coming expansion of the role of the income concept complex in society.

# 9

## 'Tis the Age of Aquarius –
## Even for Accounting

*by* MARVIN L. STONE

STONE, GRAY AND COMPANY

I RECENTLY saw a rather interesting employment application which I thought I would pass on to you. It was from a twenty-three year old young man with excellent credentials. He came from a good college. The only thing that puzzled me about him were his vital statistics. Normally, I would not pay much attention to such trivia. However, in this case, the usually perfunctory data looked a little strange. You see, his height was shown as sixteen inches and his weight as four pounds.

As I sat waiting for him to walk in that day, I mused about some of the possible engagements in which such an accountant might prove useful. I thought he might be ideal to investigate inventories on the bottom shelf, or perhaps to write footnotes in even smaller letters. You can imagine my surprise when a strapping two-hundred pounder walked through the doorway.

After a cursory discussion of his other qualifications, all of which proved eminently satisfactory, I asked him to explain the peculiarity in his vital statistics. He said he had been trained in a very good college, and he understood that generally accepted accounting principles required the presentation of all data at cost less depreciation. Interpolating this requirement to his own vital statistics, he had shown his height and weight at two-thirds of his height and weight at birth,

145

because he felt that at age twenty-three, he was about one-third depreciated.

The vital statistics in this application were just about as useful to me as historical cost data are to a reader of financial statements. Since accounting is intended to be a utilitarian art, the continued preparation of useless data is intolerable. In fact, it is downright suicidal. Our only reason for existence is the usefulness of our product. This morning, George Staubus said that he was impressed with the uselessness of balance sheets. I must say that I am depressed by the same thing.

There is ample evidence that the financial statements we presently prepare are not very useful. They are largely ignored by management, by investors, by almost everyone for whom they are prepared. Incident to the preparation of his thesis, a master's candidate at the University of Denver asked business executives and investors the extent to which they based their decisions on financial statements. He was somewhat shocked to learn that practically no one paid any attention to financial statements. To paraphrase his findings, generally accepted accounting principles seem to produce generally ignored financial statements.

This is not to say that accountants are not trying to improve their product. Certainly we are not standing still nor ignoring modern technology. Not at all. We are striving diligently to invest all of this useless data which no one wants or uses with increasing degrees of precision. Computers permit the production of useless data much faster; we are constantly improving accounting terminology so that this useless data will be more understandable; and, of course, we are improving our audit techniques tremendously so that we can make this useless data more credible.

After listening to the intense discussions during the last two days, I am sure that most of you agree that our consumers need and are entitled to receive current value financial statements. Current values, of course, mean different things to different people, as I have discovered since this symposium began. Furthermore, current value statements will not solve all of our problems. In fact, current value statements will undoubtedly create as many difficult problems as they will solve. Not the least of these new problems will be which current value to use. However, attacking these new problems is at least a useful exercise, since the effort will be expended toward a better goal—a goal of providing useful information for people who rely on us.

Accountants shudder at the non-objectivity of current values. They tend to forget just how many subjective judgments permeate the financial statements that we now prepare. Calculation of a bad debt provision, determination of an inventory's saleability, determination of the period during which benefits will be derived from research and development expenditures, the status of long-term contracts in process, even the extent and maturity of many liabilities. All of these items, and many more as well, require the exercise of subjective judgment, making cost based financial statements much less objective than their proponents claim.

Objectivity, while a desirable attribute, must not override other principles of equal importance. Unfortunately, the accountant's preoccupation with objectivity has tended to act as blinders. It is these blinders which make it possible for normally utilitarian-minded men to produce financial statements based on cost, when cost is often as meaningless a statistic as the temperature on the date of acquisition.

The use of historical cost data has become more a habit—a reflex action—than an affirmative effort at objectivity. We react much as did Yogi Berra, famed New York Yankee catcher, when he sprinted across the street just in time to catch a baby who had toppled from a third-story window and then, without even breaking stride, threw her to second base.

Of course, current values aren't ignored altogether in cost based financial statements. As Jim MacNeill pointed out, book values are adjusted downward whenever current values are lower. In such instances, accountants apparently agree that even objectivity has its limitations. Such downward adjustments are made in keeping with the overriding doctrine that financial statements must be conservative. Conservatism, too, is a worthwhile principle. However, the yardstick of conservatism was fashioned in another era—an era in which financial statements were presumed to be a report by an informed insider to an uninformed outsider, usually a creditor.

Unfortunately, conservatism has become a euphemism for undervaluation. In today's economy, financial statements are prepared for a wide variety of users. The accountant can inflict just as much damage on a prospective seller of stock by issuing an undervalued statement as he can damage a creditor by permitting management's puffing to be included in the financial statements. The present day financial statement format was an imaginative innovation when it was devised. The format came into being to meet the needs of users. However, continued slavish adherence to a form which no longer meets the needs of today's users is like building structures in 18th century style. While some people might prefer 18th century architecture for esthetic reasons (assuming environment permits), esthetics have no place in a utilitarian art like accounting.

How do we start on the road to current value financial statements; how do we bring accounting into this Aquarian Age? My first suggestion is negative rather than positive. I suggest that we do not wait for the Accounting Principles Board, or some other similarly constituted body, to produce ground rules. This is not meant as a criticism of the APB nor is it meant as an inference that it has not done or is not doing an admirable job. However, I believe that rules for this type of experimental financial statement must be developed through experimentation. Just as high heels were invented by a girl who was kissed several times on the forehead, accountants must invent statements which will meet the need of users. Our sights, too, must be raised and we must expect to miss the mark occasionally. A period of experimentation can be productive only if we keep uppermost in our minds the basic goal, and that goal should be the production of data which reflect the best estimate of current values. The importance of this basic goal has been stressed, first by George Catlett and later by others. I concur with the importance of this goal. Unless it is kept firmly in mind, we could end up with an even worse hodgepodge than we presently have.

After listening to the pros and cons of each method of valuation, I must conclude that no one valuation method is ideal for valuing all assets and liabilities, Professor Chambers' protestations notwithstanding. Nevertheless, I see nothing wrong with using whatever method seems most appropriate to value each individual asset, bearing in mind our basic goal: the presentation of the best available estimate of current values.

In the beginning, current value accounting will be unsettling to accountants who are comfortable portraying forty acres of land at its original four hundred dollar cost, even though the forty acres now happen to be downtown Dallas. Innovation and growth are always uncomfortable and unsettling. Selling the idea of current value financial statements to accountants won't be easy. Selling these new concepts to people outside of our profession will be even more difficult.

Even though data contained in historical cost financial statements are largely ignored, "users" of financial statements will still feel more comfortable with the status quo than with the unknown. Financial analysts and other users will undoubtedly express grave concern over a whole new set of unknown complexities. Managements are not likely to be overly enthusiastic with any change, since the first experimental efforts will, undoubtedly, take more time and cost more money. Farsighted managements should equate their companies' best interest with the maintenance of a well-informed investor market. However, not many managements are that farsighted. Some managements might even be concerned that the first companies to hop on the bandwagon may appear to be looking for a way to add window-dressing to their financial statements. And, of course, some will resist change for the same human reasons that affect us all.

Even though selling new concepts will not be easy, sell them we must, or be relegated to ultimate oblivion. Increasing numbers of people need and want an understandable means of evaluating corporate securities. Present financial statements are not meeting those needs. Accountants are still going down to sea in papyrus boats. This may be all right for Thor Heyerdahl, but it is the wrong posture for a dynamic profession.

Since nature abhors a vacuum, some group or groups will inevitably devise a means to communicate the desired information in a better way. Given present day technology, it is not farfetched to suppose that a group of economists, demographers, behavioral scientists and sociologists might crank into a computer a variety of data which measure a company's operations, the quality of its management, and the future potential of the company and the entire industry. Since this is the Age of Aquarius, an astrologer might even be included to incorporate his predictions. Were this computer program written by an accountant, the output could predictably be expected to be portrayed in what we laughably call "the language of business." More astute communicators, recognizing the fact that accounting is the language not of business but of accountants, will devise a more generally understood language.

For example, the output might take the form of a color spectrum on which red signified good and blue bad. Thus, the color reported by the computer would be judged by its proximity to one end or the other of the spectrum. Degrees of good or bad could be depicted by the vividness of the colors. Pink or light red could denote fairly good, while dark blue would denote very bad. Such an index would, undoubtedly, be preferred by the public over present accounting statements, even when they are condensed to that commonly used index, earnings-per-share.

Should this new system of reporting indeed become prevalent, many commonly used expressions will need revision. "Blue chips" will become "red chips." A useful by-product of this change in terminology might well be the elimination of such language discrepancies as "in the red" signifying bad while "in the pink" signifies good. "In the red" will necessarily become "in the blue." Should such a reporting system indeed come to pass, I fear the attest function could well be lost to accountants, since auditors are commonly thought to be color blind.

Now, back to current value financial statements after that brief glimpse of the future. In spite of a probable lack of enthusiasm on the part of users and managements, the publicity attendant first attempts at more meaningful financial statements might help the cause more than we might expect. Financial writers should find the conversion good copy. The publicity might even produce a groundswell of public opinion favoring more meaningful data, although, in all candor, a groundswell of apathy seems more likely. Some managements might see current value financial statements as an opportunity to improve reported earnings. They might well climb on the bandwagon early. While the inflation of reported earnings is not at all the goal toward which current value financial statements strive (in fact, the exact opposite might well result), assistance will be welcome no matter what the motivation.

Even if everyone agrees that reporting should be converted to current values, the conversion cannot possibly occur overnight. A great many transitional problems must be faced. These formidable problems might well be expected to evoke from many observers the same reaction as was received by an errant tourist motoring through the Tennessee hinterland. When he asked a farmer for the best way to get to Memphis, the farmer scratched his head slowly and then drawled: "If

I were going to Memphis, I wouldn't start here." Many critics of current value financial statements might well take the position that current values would have been a good idea when financial reporting commenced, but that the conversion now is simply impractical.

In his excellent book, Howard Ross[1] estimates that most of the transitional problems could be resolved within two years if the movement toward current value financial statements really picks up momentum. While I am not as optimistic as Howard Ross, I do feel that the conversion could take place within a reasonable period of time and further, that the rewards will be well worth the effort.

During the transitional period, current value data could be reported in a number of different ways. It might be shown, for example, as a supplement to the regular cost-based financial statements. I do not favor this method since it would tend to perpetuate cost-based financial statements indefinitely. The two-column financial statement recommended in the AICPA audit guide for personal financial statements is another method of portraying current values. In my opinion, that format is too complex. I find that most of my clients experience great difficulty understanding the two-column statements which we have prepared for them. Separate financial statements might be prepared—one set incorporating cost data and the other current value data. Eventually, the cost statement could be phased out, as users are gradually weaned away from cost data. CPAs might even report on both financial statements, although the traditional opinion language would need substantial revision before it could be used for current value statements. Ideally, current values could be reported in the regular financial statements, with cost data appended as a supplement. This, too, would require substantial change in the wording of the CPA's opinion. Eventually, the supplementary cost data could be eliminated entirely.

Even when financial statements report current values, it seems to me that the reporting entity's records must still be maintained on the basis of historical cost. Investors and other users would, thus, continue to receive the degree of assurance which Yuji Ijiri asserts is an inherent advantage of the historical cost system.

Before closing, may I again commend to your attention the writings

[1] Howard Ross, *Financial Statements: A Crusade for Current Values* (New York: Pitman Publishing Corporation, 1969).

of Howard Ross. Not only his recent book, which I cited earlier, but also his first book, *The Elusive Art of Accounting*,[2] contain the most logical and persuasive argument in favor of current values that I have seen anywhere. Further, his writing style is thoroughly delightful and a model of clarity. I have enjoyed his writings and gratefully acknowledge them as the source of many ideas I have expressed here tonight.

In closing, let me express my appreciation to all of the participants in this symposium for contributing so much to my education. The experience of the last two days has served to confirm even further my feeling that each of us should return to the college campus from time to time in order to recharge our mental batteries. All of you have added a great many new words to my vocabulary: surrogate, pejorative, eclectic, coefficient. I am still trying to construct a sentence in which all of these words are used, in order to fix them firmly in my mind.

I also appreciate the fact that you straightened out a number of misconceptions in my rather limited vocabulary. I always thought that "additive" was a gasoline ingredient. I now find that "models" are not all to be whistled at.

My education didn't come easy, though. Just when I was getting the hang of what was going on, Ray Chambers changed the ground rules by announcing that *he* believed everything he said. Obviously, he was a representative of the vociferous minority.

Finally, to all the combatants in this last day and one-half of mayhem, let me quote the Episcopalian minister who told a Baptist preacher, "There's no reason for us to argue; after all, we are all doing God's work—you in your way and I in His."

I have enjoyed doing "God's work" with you these last two days.

---

[2] Howard Ross, *The Elusive Art of Accounting: A Brash Commentary on Financial Statements* (New York: The Ronald Press Company, 1966).